Published by:

John Wiley & Sons Canada, Ltd.

6045 Freemont Blvd.
Mississauga, ON L5R 4J3

ISBN 978-0-470-67636-3

Editor: Gene Shannon
Production Editor: Pauline Ricablanca
Project Coordinator: Lynsey Stanford
Editorial Assistant: Katie Wolsley
Photo Editor: Photo Affairs, Inc.
Cartographer: Lohnes+Wright
Vice President, Publishing Services: Karen Bryan
Production by Wiley Indianapolis Composition Services

For information on our other products and services or to obtain technical support, please contact our Customer Care Department within the U.S. at 877/762-2974, outside the U.S. at 317/572-3993 or fax 317/572-4002.

Wiley also publishes its books in a variety of electronic formats. Some content that appears in print may not be available in electronic formats.

Manufactured in China

1 2 3 4 5 RRD 14 13 12 11 10

915.6944
F932d
2010
KGL

Fron

Includes 1 Map

Jerusalem
day BY day™

1st Edition

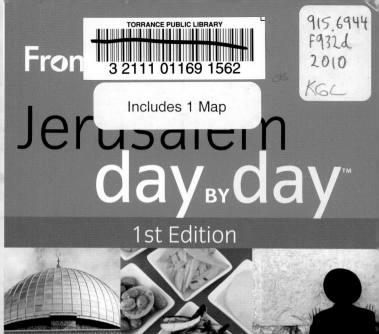

by Buzzy Gordon

John Wiley & Sons Canada, Ltd.

Contents

A Note from the Editorial Director

Organizing your time. That's what this guide is all about.

Other guides give you long lists of things to see and do and then expect you to fit the pieces together. The Day by Day guides are different. These guides tell you the best of everything, and then they show you how to see it *in the smartest, most time-efficient way*. Our authors have designed detailed itineraries organized by time, neighborhood, or special interest. And each tour comes with a bulleted map that takes you from stop to stop.

Hoping to walk the Via Dolorosa or visit the Temple Mount? Planning a swim in the Dead Sea or a stroll through the markets of Mahane Yehuda? Whatever your interest or schedule, the Day by Days give you the smartest routes to follow. Not only do we take you to the top attractions, hotels, and restaurants, but we also help you access those special moments that locals get to experience—those "finds" that turn tourists into travelers.

The Day by Days are also your top choice if you're looking for one complete guide for all your travel needs. The best hotels and restaurants for every budget, the greatest shopping values, the wildest nightlife—it's all here.

Why should you trust our judgment? Because our authors personally visit each place they write about. They're an independent lot who say what they think and would never include places they wouldn't recommend to their best friends. They're also open to suggestions from readers. If you'd like to contact them, please send your comments our way at feedback@frommers.com, and we'll pass them on.

Enjoy your Day by Day guide—the most helpful travel companion you can buy. And have the trip of a lifetime.

Warm regards,

Kelly Regan

Kelly Regan, Editorial Director
Frommer's Travel Guides

About the Author

Award-winning journalist **Buzzy Gordon** has been a travel columnist for *USA Today* and an editor at *The Jerusalem Post*. His work has appeared in such prominent publications as *National Geographic Traveler, The Los Angeles Times,* and *The Washington Post.* He is a regular contributor to leading international travel websites.

Acknowledgments

The author would like to thank Carol Smith, Ronna Katz, and Danby Meital for their invaluable assistance.

This book is dedicated to the loving memory of my parents, who made Jerusalem their home for the best years of their lives and imparted their love of the city to me.

An Additional Note

Please be advised that travel information is subject to change at any time—and this is especially true of prices. We therefore suggest that you write or call ahead for confirmation when making your travel plans. The authors, editors, and publisher cannot be held responsible for the experiences of readers while traveling. Your safety is important to us, however, so we encourage you to stay alert and be aware of your surroundings.

Star Ratings, Icons & Abbreviations

Every hotel, restaurant, and attraction listing in this guide has been ranked for quality, value, service, amenities, and special features using a **star-rating system.** Hotels, restaurants, attractions, shopping, and nightlife are rated on a scale of zero stars (recommended) to three stars (exceptional). In addition to the star-rating system, we also use a **kids icon** to point out the best bets for families. Within each tour, we recommend cafes, bars, or restaurants where you can take a break. Each of these stops appears in a shaded box marked with a coffee-cup-shaped bullet.

The following **abbreviations** are used for credit cards:

AE	American Express	DISC	Discover	V	Visa
DC	Diners Club	MC	MasterCard		

Frommers.com

Now that you have this guidebook to help you plan a great trip, visit our web-site at **www.frommers.com** for additional travel information on more than 4,000 destinations. We update features regularly to give you instant access to the most current trip-planning information available. At Frommers.com, you'll find scoops on the best airfares, lodging rates, and car rental bargains. You can even book your travel online through our reliable travel booking partners. Other popular features include:

- Online updates of our most popular guidebooks
- Vacation sweepstakes and contest giveaways
- Newsletters highlighting the hottest travel trends
- Podcasts, interactive maps, and up-to-the-minute events listings
- Opinionated blog entries by Arthur Frommer himself
- Online travel message boards with featured travel discussions

A Note on Prices

In the "Take a Break" and "Best Bets" sections of this book, we have used a system of dollar signs to show a range of costs for 1 night in a hotel (the price of a double-occupancy room) or the cost of an entree at a restaurant. Use the following table to decipher the dollar signs:

Cost	Hotels	Restaurants
$	under $100	under $10
$$	$100–$200	$10–$20
$$$	$200–$300	$20–$30
$$$$	$300–$400	$30–$40
$$$$$	over $400	over $40

An Invitation to the Reader

In researching this book, we discovered many wonderful places—hotels, restaurants, shops, and more. We're sure you'll find others. Please tell us about them, so we can share the information with your fellow travelers in upcoming editions. If you were disappointed with a recommendation, we'd love to know that, too. Please write to:

Frommer's Jerusalem Day by Day, 1st Edition
John Wiley & Sons Canada, Ltd. • 6045 Freemont Blvd. • Mississauga, ON L5R 4J3

16 Favorite **Moments**

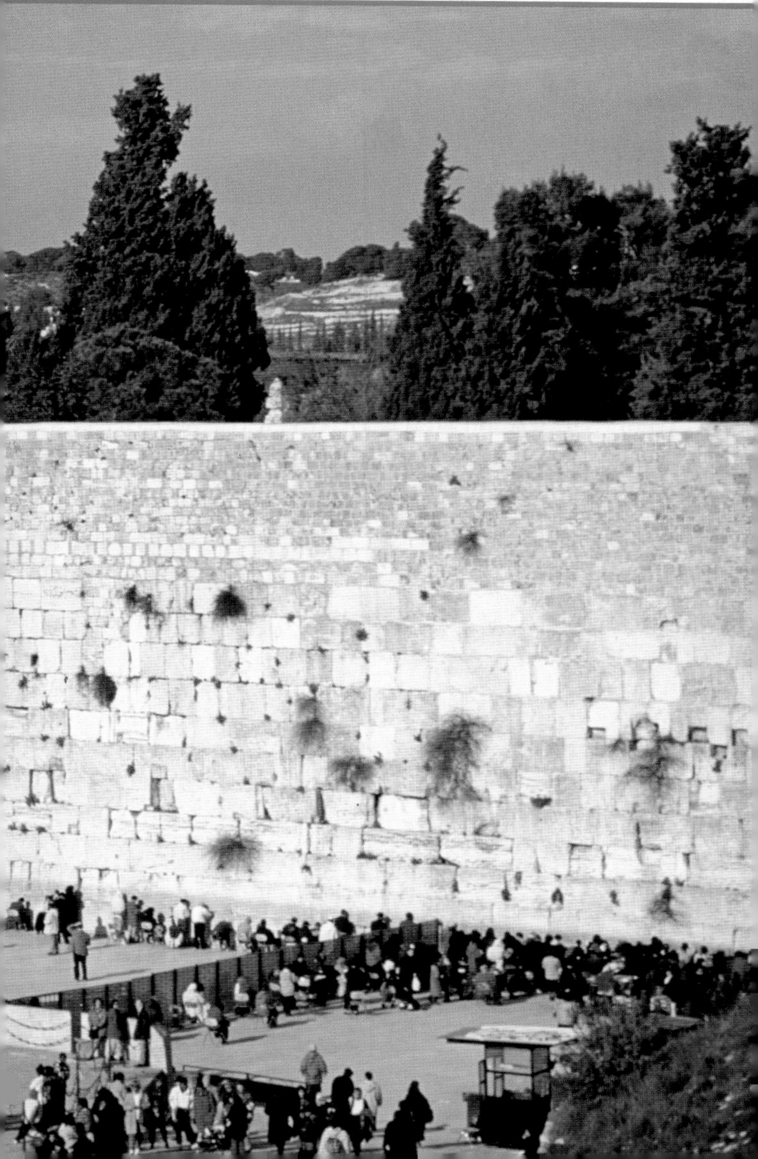

16 Favorite **Moments**

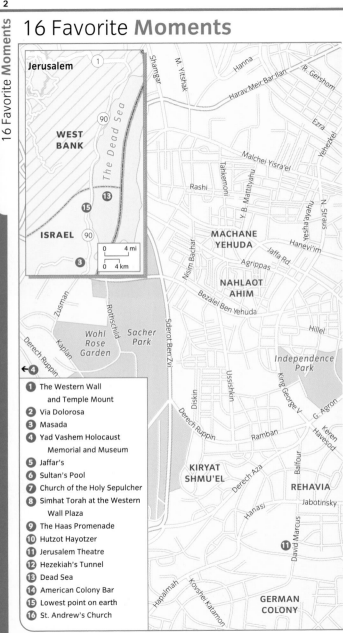

Jerusalem

WEST BANK

The Dead Sea

ISRAEL

| 0 | 4 mi |
| 0 | 4 km |

M. Ytshak

Shamgar

Hanna

Harav Meir Bar Ilan

R. Gershom

Ezra

Yehezkel

Malchei Yisra'el

Tahkemoni

Rashi

Y. B. Mattityahu

N. Straus

Yesha'ayahu

MACHANE YEHUDA

Hanevi'im

Jaffa Rd

Agrippas

NAHLAOT AHIM

Bezalel Ben Yehuda

Hillel

Zusman

Rothschild

Kaplan

Wohl Rose Garden

Sacher Park

Sderot Ben Zvi

Independence Park

King George V

G. Agron

Keren Havesod

Derech Ruppin

Diskin

Ussishkin

Derech Ruppin

Ramban

Balfour

KIRYAT SHMU'EL

Derech Aza

Hanasi

REHAVIA

Jabotinsky

David Marcus

Hapalmah

Kovshei Katamon

GERMAN COLONY

1. The Western Wall and Temple Mount
2. Via Dolorosa
3. Masada
4. Yad Vashem Holocaust Memorial and Museum
5. Jaffar's
6. Sultan's Pool
7. Church of the Holy Sepulcher
8. Simhat Torah at the Western Wall Plaza
9. The Haas Promenade
10. Hutzot Hayotzer
11. Jerusalem Theatre
12. Hezekiah's Tunnel
13. Dead Sea
14. American Colony Bar
15. Lowest point on earth
16. St. Andrew's Church

Previous page: An overview of the Dome of the Rock and the Western Wall.

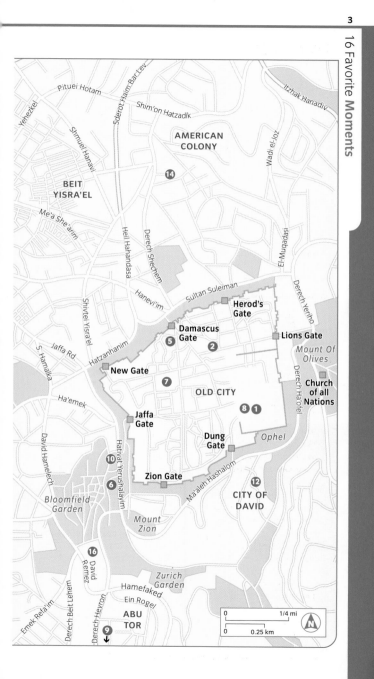

Pituei Hotam
Shim'on Hatzadik
Itzhak Hanadiv
Yeherzkel
Shmuel Hanavi
Sderot Haim Bar Lev

AMERICAN
COLONY

Wadi el-Joz

BEIT
YISRA'EL

14

Me'a She'arim

Derech Shechem
Heil Hahandasa

El-Muqadasi

Hanevi'im
Sultan Suleiman

Herod's
Gate

Derech Yeriho

Shivtei Yisra'el

Jaffa Rd.

Damascus
Gate

5   2

Lions Gate

Hatzanhanim
New Gate

Mount Of
Olives

S. Hamalka

7

Derech Ha'ofel

Ha'emek
OLD CITY

Church
of all
Nations

Jaffa
Gate

8 1

David Hamelech

Dung
Gate

Ophel

10

Zion Gate

Ma'aleh Hashalom

6

12

Bloomfield
Garden

Mount
Zion

CITY OF
DAVID

16

David Remez

Zurich
Garden

Emek Refa'im

Hamefaked

Ein Rogel

Derech Beit Lehem

ABU
TOR

Derech Hevron

9
↓

0   1/4 mi
0   0.25 km

N

As the eternal city sacred to three great religions, Jerusalem is unparalleled in its opportunities for uplifting spiritual experiences and communing with history. But it is also a modern, vibrant city where the cuisines and cultures of Arabs and Jews, enhanced by the influence of immigrants from Russia to South America, add infinite variety to the fabric of the city.

1 Saying a prayer at the Western Wall and Temple Mount. This revered complex comprises sites that are holy to all three Western monotheistic religions. Jews come here to stuff notes of supplication between the stones of the lone wall remaining from Solomon's Temple, where Jesus confronted the money-lenders and Muhammad is said to have ascended to heaven. You don't need to be devoutly religious to feel the incredible spiritual energy of this enduring remnant of the ancient temple. *See p 9.*

2 Witnessing Holy Week in the Christian Quarter. The processions of a joyful Palm Sunday and sorrowful Good Friday along the Via Dolorosa are moving acts of faith that attract pilgrims and observers from

The crowd bears a crucifix along the Via Dolorosa on Good Friday.

all over the world. Practically every day of the week, penitents bear crosses from one Station of the Cross to the next. *See p 12.*

3 Exploring Masada. King Herod's cliff-top fortress and site of Jewish defenders' last stand against the Romans in 73 CE—where they chose death by suicide instead of surrender and slavery—has become the enduring symbol of Israeli bravery. If you are in good shape, consider climbing up the Snake Path to watch the sunrise over the Dead Sea. The nighttime sound-and-light show dramatizing the defenders' last weeks will also leave a lasting—and chilling—impression. *See p 143.*

4 Remembering at the Yad Vashem Holocaust Memorial and Museum. You'll need time to recover after visiting the most haunting and comprehensive of the world's tributes to the 6 million Jews murdered by the Nazis during World War II, but it is an important lesson for teens and adults of all faiths. Traditionally, every foreign dignitary visiting Israel lays a wreath here (like official visitors to the United States do at the Tomb of the Unknown Soldier). *See p 28.*

5 Sampling kanaffeh in the Arab bazaar. It is impossible to compare the taste of this pastry—which combines a mild cheese with a sweet, crispy topping—with anything you have ever eaten before. The best place to try it is Jaffar's (in Suq Khan ez-Zeit Bazaar), near Damascus Gate.

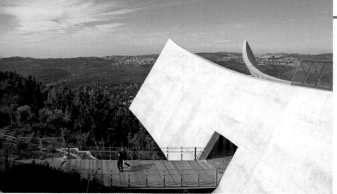

The exit of the Yad Vashem Holocaust Memorial and Museum, designed by architect Moshe Safdie.

⑥ Attending a performance at Sultan's Pool. This sprawling outdoor amphitheater, incorporating the natural topography at the foot of the Old City walls, is an unforgettable venue for an evening show, whether it is a concert featuring international rock stars, a symphony orchestra under the baton of a famous conductor, or an opera staged by one of the world's great companies. *See p 124.*

⑦ Marveling at the Orthodox Easter fire ceremony. Celebrated annually at the Church of the Holy Sepulcher, the Greek Orthodox Easter nocturnal fire rite is one of the most vibrant and extraordinary Christian observances in the religious calendar. A torch lit inside the sanctuary is paraded by the throng through the streets of the Old City. *See p 12.*

⑧ Accompanying Torah Scrolls during the festival of Simhat Torah. To celebrate the end—and beginning again—of the yearly cycle of weekly Torah readings, Jewish revelers dance through the city streets to the Western Wall while holding aloft richly adorned Torah scrolls. This caps off the week-long Succot (Festival of Booths). (The holiday falls in the Hebrew month of Tishrei, right after Yom Kippur (Day of Atonement), corresponding with Sept or Oct.)

⑨ Viewing the Old City from the Haas Promenade. The fading sunlight hitting the stone of the ancient walls and glinting off the Dome of the Rock gives the city its designation "Jerusalem of Gold." Wait for the street lights to twinkle on. For those who love the panorama, it should also be experienced from the Mt. of Olives. *See p 14.*

⑩ Browsing works of art at Hutzot Hayotzer. The Hutzot Hayotzer artists' quarter opposite Jaffa Gate is open all year round, but the time to go is during each summer's international crafts fair, when you can admire and purchase crafts and handiwork (such as pottery, ceramics, and weaving) from around the world. You can also sample many different ethnic snack foods and desserts while enjoying folklore shows from everywhere from South America to Asia. *See p 88.*

⑪ Enjoying the best of international culture at the Israel Festival. Held every May to June, this prestigious arts and entertainment festival brings world-class concerts,

A woman floats in the Dead Sea while reading a magazine.

plays, and shows to the Jerusalem Theatre and other major auditoriums. There are also free events held at outdoor venues. *See p 162*.

⑫ Walking through Hezekiah's Tunnel. It can be a little taxing to make your way—frequently while crouching by candlelight or mini-flashlight—through this underground water conduit into the ancient city, but it is an intriguing way to relive history and gain an appreciation for a feat of engineering dating back 2 millennia. *See p 18*.

⑬ Floating in the Dead Sea. Bob like a cork—or even recline while reading a newspaper—on the surface of the world's most buoyant body of water. The salty lake's minerals have also been shown to impart healthful benefits. *See p 144*.

⑭ Toasting romance at the American Colony Bar. Enjoy a drink with that special someone in an intimate Middle Eastern atmosphere reminiscent of Bogey and Bergman in Casablanca. *See p 134*.

⑮ Posing for a photo at the lowest place on Earth. Have your picture taken at a true geographic landmark: next to the sign indicating that you are standing 416m (1,365 ft.) below sea level, the lowest land altitude on the planet. *See p 144*.

⑯ Listening to music in an old church with incredible acoustics. Israel is blessed with many venerable churches (like St. Anne's and Dormition Abbey in the Old City, and St. Andrew's in West Jerusalem) where concerts of classical and sacred music resonate in chapels and caverns possessing remarkable acoustical properties. Catch a regularly scheduled weekly performance or plan to attend one of the semi-annual liturgical music festivals in the chapels of Abu Gosh. *See p 40*. ●

The Best **Full-Day Tours**

The Best in **One Day**

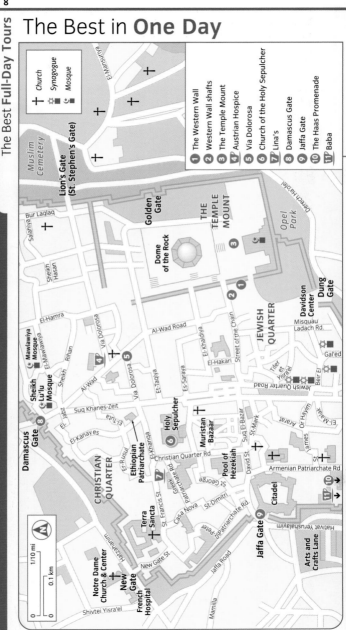

Legend
+ Church
✡ Synagogue
☪ Mosque

1 The Western Wall
2 Western Wall shafts
3 The Temple Mount
4 Austrian Hospice
5 Via Dolorosa
6 Church of the Holy Sepulcher
7 Lina's
8 Damascus Gate
9 Jaffa Gate
10 The Haas Promenade
11 Baba

Muslim Cemetery

Lion's Gate (St. Stephen's Gate)

Golden Gate

THE TEMPLE MOUNT

Opel Park

Bur Laqlaq

Salahiya

Sheikh Hasan

Dome of the Rock

El-Mansuriya

El-Hamra

Mawlawiya Mosque
El-Mawlawiya

Via Dolorosa

Sheikh Lu'lu Mosque

Rihan

Sheikh

El-Jabz

Al-Wad

Via Dolorosa

Al-Wad Road

El-Khaldiya

El-Hakari

El-Tura

Et-Taqiya

Es-Saraya

JEWISH QUARTER

Street of the Chain

Davidson Center

Dung Gate

Misqau Ladach Rd.

Gal'ed

Tifer El Yisrael

Jewish Quarter Road

Beit El

Suq Khanes-Zeit

Damascus Gate

El-Kanayes

Holy Sepulcher

Muristan Bazaar

Suq El-Bazar

St-Mark

Or Hayim

Ararat

El-Malak

CHRISTIAN QUARTER

Ethiopian Patriarchate

Christian Quarter Rd.

St George

Pool of Hezekiah

St-Dimitri

David St.

St James

Armenian Patriarchate Rd

Er-Rusul

El-Khanqa

Greek Rd

Casa Patriarchate Rd

Terra Sancta

St. Francis St.

Casa Nova

St-Peter

Citadel

Jaffa Gate

Notre Dame Church & Center

New Gate

French Hospital

Habad

Jaffa Road

St-Patriarchate Rd.

Hativat Yerushalayim

Arts and Crafts Lane

New Gate St.

Shivtei Yisra'el

Mamilla

Derech Ha'ofel

1/10 mi
0.1 km

Previous page: Walking along the Western Wall shafts.

Day 1 focuses almost exclusively on the Old City, which contains most of the historic and sacred sites for which Jerusalem is justly famous as a pilgrimage destination for Jews, Christians, and Muslims. We start with the Western Wall, which is an integral part of the Temple Mount revered by all three religions. City Tour Bus 99 (see p 15) is recommended as a traveling observation platform from which to view and gain perspective of both the Old and New cities—before ending up at the Haas Promenade, the stationary outlook providing the most comprehensive panorama of the walled city. START: **Dung Gate.**

Travel Tip

Cabs are the way to go to get between stops on this tour—less expensive than renting a car and almost as cheap as public transit for two people. In wintertime, there are fewer daylight hours before sunset, when you want to be at the end of the tour. Take a hat and drinking water, no matter what the season.

❶ ★★★ The Western Wall.

Known in Hebrew as *HaKotel HaMa'aravi* (or simply the Kotel), it has also been called the "Wailing Wall," since Jews here mourn the loss of their Temple. This is the holiest of Jewish sites, a sizable remnant of the monumental retaining wall that still supports the Temple Mount. After 1948, when the Old City was controlled by Jordan, Jews were denied access to this site; since 1967, Israeli policy has been to permit free access to worship for all religions at all holy sites. Visitors of all religious faiths are welcome to approach the Wall to pray, meditate, or stuff a small note into a crack between the stones; these "messages to God" (Pope Benedict XVI [1927–] delivered one) are collected monthly. Men must wear a hat or head covering; simple ones

Men praying at the Western Wall.

The Al Aqsa Mosque at the Temple Mount.

are available at no cost from a box beside the entrance to the prayer area. Women should be modestly dressed. The right-hand section of the Wall Plaza is for women, who are not allowed in the men's section (as per Orthodox Jewish tradition); however, a man and woman (or family) can pray together at the Wall on their respective sides of the barrier. Smoking is disrespectful in the prayer area; no photography is permitted on the Sabbath and most Jewish holidays. ⏱ *1 hr. Free admission.*

② ★★ **Western Wall shafts.** The Wall is actually much deeper and longer than the part we can readily see today; for an idea of the original, enter the doorway located between the men's restrooms and the public telephones on the plaza's northern side; shafts have been sunk along the Wall to show its true depth and ground levels in Herodian and Crusader times. ⏱ *½ hr. Admission NIS 25 adults, NIS 15 children &*

*seniors. Sun–Thurs 8am–dusk, Fri & eve of festivals 7am–noon; closed Sat & most Jewish holidays. Tours can be arranged by making an appointment with the Western Wall Generations Center (☎ *5958, http://english.thekotel.org).*

Travel Tip

The 4-digit phone number, preceded by a *, is a dialing shortcut that many companies provide for the convenience of their customers.

③ ★★ **The Temple Mount.** Israel has turned over control of the Temple Mount and its mosques to the Muslim Religious Authority *(the Waqf)*, except for maintaining security. Access (up the ramp from the Western Wall Plaza) is free of charge. It is sacred to Jews as the site of ancient Israel's Temples and to Muslims as the place from which Muhammad ascended to Heaven.

Temple Mount

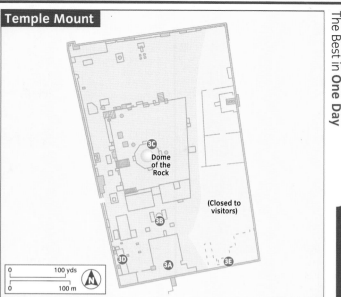

Dome
of the
Rock

(Closed to
visitors)

3A 3B 3C 3D 3E

0   100 yds
0   100 m

3A ★ **Al Aqsa Mosque** is the third-holiest place of prayer for Muslims after Mecca and Medina. To the southeast of the building is a corner in the Temple Mount walls; some say this is the "pinnacle of the Temple" where Satan took Jesus to tempt him. From here is a view of the Mount of Olives and its churches. **3B** ★★ **El-Kas** is the fountain with faucets where Muslims perform their ritual ablutions; the circular row of pink marble seats is off-limits to non-Muslims. The exterior of the **3C** ★★★ **Dome of the Rock** was tiled by Sultan Suleiman (1520–1566) in the 16th century. In 1994, Jordan's King Hussein (1935–1999) had the dome gilded with 24-karat gold. Jews and

Muslims believe the rock housed within is the altar where Abraham almost sacrificed his son Isaac. The Waqf frequently closes the interiors of the Al Aqsa Mosque and Dome of the Rock (as well as the Islamic Museum **3D** and Solomon's Stables **3E**) to tourists. ⏱ *½ hr. plus possibly up to 1 hr. waiting time in line. May to Oct, Sun–Thurs 7:30–11am & 1:30–2:30pm, Nov to Apr, Sun–Thurs 7:30–10am & 11:30am–1:30pm; best to arrive an hour ahead of closing time. The Temple Mount is closed to non-Muslims on Fri (the Muslim Sabbath) & Muslim holidays; it is open only morning hours during the holy month of Ramadan. Modest dress is enforced; even men with shorts too short may be denied admission.*

Leaving the Western Wall Plaza along Al-Wad Street to the north will bring you to the **4** **Austrian Hospice** at the eastern edge of the Via Dolorosa. The coffee shop, located in a garden, is a remarkably tranquil oasis in the relative austerity of the Old City; it is justifiably famous for its delicious apple strudel. Kosher food options can be found on the Jewish Quarter side of the Plaza. *37 Via Dolorosa 37.* ☎ *02/626-5800. $.*

5 ★★★ **Via Dolorosa.** The Latin literally means Sorrowful Path, traditionally believed to be the Way of the Cross followed by Jesus bearing the instrument of his death to Calvary, the site of the Crucifixion. Over the centuries, millions of pilgrims have come here to walk the way their Lord trod and to pray at the 14 Stations of the Cross. The Via Dolorosa begins in the Muslim Quarter, in the northeast corner of the Old City, and winds its way to the Church of the Holy Sepulcher in the Christian Quarter. Each Station is marked by a small sign or a number engraved in the stone lintel over a door. Paving stones on the Via

Dolorosa itself—most of whose route coincides with the alleys of the Arab *souk,* or bazaar—have been set in a semicircular pattern to mark those Stations directly on the street. Other Stations are behind closed doors; knock and someone will probably be there to open up for you. Each Friday at 4pm, monks lead a procession for pilgrims, some carrying crosses, along the Via Dolorosa. (See p 39, **1** and sidebar, for details and descriptions of the Stations.) There are free restrooms at several spots along the route. ⏱ *1 hr. The Via Dolorosa never closes, but it is not advisable to be here at night.*

6 ★★★ **Church of the Holy Sepulcher.** The church contains the last four Stations of the Via Dolorosa and is divided among the six oldest Christian sects: Roman Catholic, Armenian Orthodox, Greek Orthodox, Egyptian Coptic, Ethiopian, and Syrian Orthodox. Each denomination has its own space (down to lines drawn in the middle of floors and pillars) and schedule of times to be in other areas of the church. The oft-changing partitioned interior is a mixture of Byzantine

Nuns along the Via Dolorosa.

traditions. Most notable are the Service of the Holy Fire (See p 5, **7**), the dramatic pageant called the Washing of the Feet, and the exotic midnight Ethiopian procession on the part of the church under Ethiopian jurisdiction—the roof. Modest dress required. 🕐 *1 hr.* ☎ *02/627-3314. Free admission. Open daily May to Oct, 5am–9pm, Nov to Apr, 4am–8pm.*

The Church of the Holy Sepulcher is divided among the six oldest Christian sects.

and Frankish Crusader styles. Inside the church are the Stone of Unction, the marble slab where the body of Jesus was prepared for burial; the site of Calvary (the second floor); and a later marble tomb enclosing the Cave of the Sepulcher. The church has been restored and is constantly being renovated. During Easter week, one can observe fascinating services held here that are based on ancient Eastern church

Time to taste the most popular dish in the Middle East—hummus. Israelis never tire of arguing which place makes the best hummus in Jerusalem: Abu Shukri or Lina's. I recommend **7** **Lina's,** where one bowl of hummus with either fava beans or whole chickpeas (and maybe a small side of falafel) mopped up with complimentary fresh pita and raw vegetables should be enough for two people to share—especially since dessert is de rigueur. Wash the hummus down with either fruit juice, lemonade, or mint tea; beer works better but is verboten on the Muslim side of town. *Lina's, 42 Ikbat a-Hanaka St. (near Station VIII of the Cross on Via Dolorosa).* ☎ *02/627-7230. $$.*

Dressing Modestly in Jerusalem

It is a good idea in Jerusalem to be prepared to be dressed "modestly" in order to avoid any unpleasantness at holy places (churches, mosques, synagogues, and the Western Wall/Temple Mount), or if you wander into an ultra-Orthodox Jewish neighborhood or pass a church that looks worth a peek inside. Women are generally fine with sleeves that are at least elbow-length and skirts to the knees (or pants that are not tight-fitting). In the hotter months, if clothing is skimpier than this, it is a good idea to carry around a long scarf (an Arab *kafiyyeh*—headdress—works fine) to cover shoulders and upper arms and a wraparound long skirt (sometimes these things can be borrowed at entrances). Men can usually get by with short sleeves and Bermuda shorts (although shorts that convert into long pants might be a worthwhile investment).

A market stall near the Damascus Gate.

8 ★★ **Damascus Gate and the bazaars.** Inside Damascus Gate, the largest of the entrances to the Old City, are cafes, shops, and market stalls lining a wide-stepped entrance street going downhill. Whether you take El-Wad (the Valley) Road to the left or Suq Khan es-Zeit (the Olive Oil Inn Market) to the right, the way becomes narrower and confusing. Unlike the markets near the Jaffa Gate, which cater primarily to tourists, this part of the bazaar is an authentic market used by the people of East Jerusalem. Suq Khan es-Zeit eventually becomes the covered Suq el Attarin, or Spice Bazaar. On the southern side of David Street, the bazaar morphs into the restored Cardo (see p 26), the main street of Roman and Byzantine Jerusalem, which runs through the rehabilitated Jewish Quarter. 🕐 *1 hr. Avoid this area at night.*

9 ★★ **Jaffa Gate.** The exterior of the magnificent Jaffa Gate merges into the outer section of the Tower of David to create the most photographed and recognizable panorama of the Old City walls when viewed from the west. The gate took on its present form when it was widened by the Ottoman rulers of Jerusalem to accommodate the pilgrimage in 1898 of Germany's Kaiser Wilhelm II (1859–1941). The walls of Jerusalem, like the city itself, are composed of stones used again and again by successive civilizations and populations. Inside the gate, on the left, is Jerusalem's main Tourist Information Office (☎ 02/627-1422; www.goisrael.com), where visitors can pick up free maps and informative literature. 🕐 *½ hr.*

10 ★★★ kids **The Haas Promenade.** The perfect way to cap any day of sightseeing in Jerusalem is to watch the city transform itself at

The Jaffa Gate.

Round-the-City Tour on Bus 99

Egged's (☎ *2800; www.egged.co.il/eng) red double-decker bus (#99) travels a continuous route, making 28 stops at most major sites throughout the united city; it is an unbeatable way to get oriented in Jerusalem. (Egged is the public sector company that operates Jerusalem's city buses.) Personal earphones give audio explanations in eight languages. *One may board at any stop, although it is best to start at the Central Bus Station. The fare for the entire route is NIS 45 for adults; all-day passes allowing hop-on, hop-off privileges are NIS 65 for adults, but you have to coordinate reentering the bus with the route schedule. Tickets may be bought at many hotels (your hotel can also make a reservation for you, advisable during peak tourist seasons) or from the driver. The bus does not run late on Friday afternoons or at all on Saturdays.*

Travelers can hop on and off of Bus 99 to get around the city.

dusk. Arguably the best vantage point is from the *tayelet*—promenade—that runs along the first ridge south of the Temple Mount. The promontory at the eastern edge of the ridge is known to the Christian world as the Hill of Evil Counsel, where the high priest Caiaphus determined to condemn Jesus. Catch Jerusalem in all its glory while it is still light out, then stand transfixed as the walls turn a golden hue as the sun begins to set. Stay until the electric lights begin to twinkle on, then head for dinner. *Daniel Yanovsky St.*

A good place for an introduction to Israeli cuisine is 🍴 ★ **Baba**; the menu provides informative explanations in English of popular Jerusalem dishes. Lamb and chicken are good choices here. *31 Emek Refaim St.* ☎ *02/566-2671. $$.*

The Best in **Two Days**

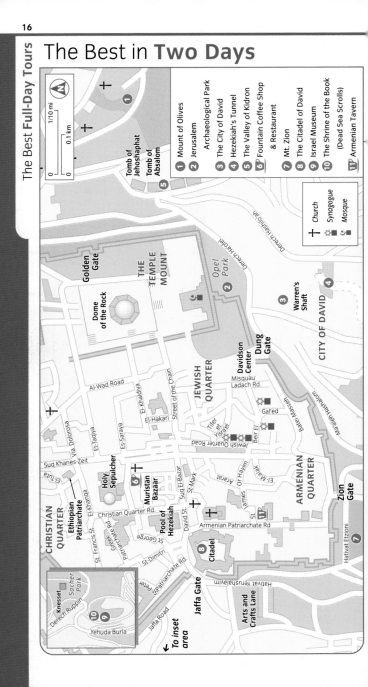

1/10 mi
0.1 km

1 Mount of Olives
2 Jerusalem
   Archaeological Park
3 The City of David
4 Hezekiah's Tunnel
5 The Valley of Kidron
6 Fountain Coffee Shop
   & Restaurant
7 Mt. Zion
8 The Citadel of David
9 Israel Museum
10 The Shrine of the Book
   (Dead Sea Scrolls)
11 Armenian Tavern

+ Church
☼ Synagogue
☾■ Mosque

Tomb of
Jehoshaphat
Tomb of
Absalom

Golden
Gate

THE
TEMPLE
MOUNT

Dome
of the Rock

Opel
Park

Warren's
Shaft

CITY OF DAVID

Davidson
Center

Dung
Gate

Al-Wad Road

El-Khaldiya

Street of the Chain

JEWISH
QUARTER

Misquau
Ladach Rd.

Derech Haofel

Derech Hashiloah

Gal'ed

Et-Taqiya

El-Hakari

Es-Saraya

Tifer
er
Yisrael

Beit El

Jewish Quarter Road

Ma'alen Hashalom

Bate Mahasse

Suq Khanes-Zeit

Via Dolorosa

El-Tuta

CHRISTIAN
QUARTER

Ethiopian
Patriarchate

St. Francis St.

El-Khanqa

Greek Rd.

Patriarchate Rd.

Christian Quarter Rd.

Holy
Sepulcher

Muristan
Bazaar

Pool of
Hezekiah

Suq El-Bazar

St-Mark

David St.

Ararat

Or Hayim

El-Ma'ak

James

St.

ARMENIAN
QUARTER

Armenian Patriarchate Rd

Zion
Gate

St George

St-Dimitri

Spatriarchate Rd.

S-Peter

Citadel

Jaffa Gate

Jaffa Road

Arts and
Crafts Lane

Hativat Yerushalayim

Hativat Etzioni

Knesset

Sacher
Park

Derech Ruppin

Yehuda Burla

To inset
area

A second day in Jerusalem lets us delve deeper into history, as revealed by startling archaeological excavations at a number of sites in and around the Old City. It's here that the past touches the present day, as you gaze upon the Dead Sea Scrolls or the room where Jesus is thought to have gathered with his disciples for the Last Supper. West Jerusalem can best be explored with a Bus 99 hop-on, hop-off ticket. START: **Mount of Olives.**

① ★★★ **Mount of Olives.** The holiest places to Christians outside the walled city are found on the slopes of this famous hill. It is revered as well by Muslims (as an apocalyptic site) and Jews, whose oldest cemetery in continuous use (except for 1949–1967, when the Jordanians encouraged its desecration) covers the slopes. The views, both in the direction of the city and the Judean Desert, are stunning. ⏱ ½ hr. See Mount of Olives & Mount Scopus, p 90.

② ★★★ **Jerusalem Archaeological Park.** The Jerusalem Archaeological Park consists primarily of the excavations at the Ophel, below the Southern Wall of the Temple Mount. In the era just preceding and during Jesus's ministry, this was the main route to the sacred enclosure. A broad staircase led to the Hulda Gates, through which pilgrims would have proceeded through tunnels to the Temple courtyard. Visitors can stand on the Broad Stairs; explore Roman-era remains; and see where the great staircase to the Temple Mount once stood, supported by a series of arches that spanned the market street below. The picture becomes clear at the park's Davidson Exhibition Center, whose virtual tour depicts the area as archaeologists believe it might have appeared in Jesus's time. Located in the ruins of an 8th-century Islamic palace, the Davidson Center contains a small museum with artifacts found at the site, as well as videos and computer information on the Temple Mount's history. ⏱ 1½ hr. Entrance between the Western Wall Plaza & Dung Gate. ☎ 02/627-7550. www.archpark.org. il. NIS 30 adults; NIS 16 students, children, & seniors. Sun–Thurs 8am–5pm, Fri 8am–2pm; closed Sat &

Visitors can explore Roman-era remains at the Jerusalem Archaeological Park.

HolyPass—The Discount Pass for Jerusalem Sites

Visitors to Jerusalem can save some money by purchasing a HolyPass, which grants admission to five sites in the Old City (two "main" sites/attractions and three "secondary" ones). The pass costs NIS 99 for adults and NIS 50 for children. Once activated (upon its first use), the HolyPass is valid for 90 days. You may inquire at the Jaffa Gate Tourist Information Office about the Holy-Pass or visit www.holypass.co.il.

Jewish holidays. 1-hr. audio tours of the center & park are available.

3 ★★ **The City of David.** It was to this area that King David, after conquering the city and claiming it from the Jebusites, brought the Ark of the Covenant—the pivotal first step in Jerusalem's transformation into a holy city and the capital of Judah/Israel; here the ark rested until King Solomon built the Temple to house it. The City of David is now the scene of the most exciting archaeological discoveries to shed light on Biblical history. ⏱ *1–2 hr. The excavations & observation*

Hezekiah's Tunnel dates from the 8th century BCE.

points of the City of David Archaeological Park are just downhill southeast from Dung Gate. ☎ 02/626-2341 or *6033. http://cityofdavid. org.il. Free admission. Daily tours in English (which may be booked in advance) cost NIS 55 & include Hezekiah's Tunnel (see below, **4**) & a 3D movie. Sun–Thurs 9am–7pm, Fri 9am–3pm.

4 ★★ **Hezekiah's Tunnel.** In the 8th century BCE, King Hezekiah constructed an underground aqueduct through which the spring water that Jerusalem depended on could be hidden from Assyrian and Babylonian invaders—an extraordinary engineering feat for the time. The tunnel is still there—along with the **Siloam Pool,** whence water was drawn for Temple rituals—waiting for you to wade through it. The one-way journey through ankle-deep water (higher on children) takes about 40 minutes; bring water-friendly footwear of some kind. There is a shorter "dry" route that gives you almost the same feeling. Visitors exiting the tunnel need not climb back uphill; there is a frequent shuttle bus costing an extra NIS 5 (pay the driver). *Entrance to the tunnel is from the City of David Archaeological Park. See* **3** *for phone number, website, open hours & fees.*

foot of the City of David and right in the middle of the present-day Arab neighborhood of Silwan—lies the vital **Gihon Spring** (known to Christians as the Fountain of the Virgin), Jerusalem's only water source from pre-Biblical times until the Ottoman Empire. There are many ancient burial caves in this "Valley of God's Judgment," and several elaborate tombs, most of which can be viewed quite adequately from vantage points on the Temple Mount and City of David. Archaeology buffs may turn to p 37 to get up close to these monuments. *Admission to the Siloam Pool NIS 12 adults.*

An excavation in the Valley of Kidron.

⑤ ★★ **The Valley of Kidron.** This narrow valley, also known as the Valley of Jehoshaphat, runs between the Mt. of Olives and the walls of the Old City, extending past the City of David southward to join with the (east-west) Valley of Hinnom and end together at the Hill of Evil Counsel (known to some as the Mount of Contempt), where Caiaphas is said to have resolved to put Jesus to death (the regional headquarters of the United Nations sits there today). In this valley—at the

In the vicinity of the Old City, Arabic fare is the logical choice for lunch. There is much more to eat than hummus: Middle Eastern salads and grilled meats, such as kebab and shwarma, can be sampled at the ⑥ ★ **Fountain Coffee Shop & Restaurant.** *Suq Efthemios Dabbagha No. 62, Christian Quarter.* ☎ *02/628-2191. $$.*

⑦ ★★ **Mt. Zion.** Mt. Zion, which dominates the southwest corner of the Old City, is home to several important Christian sites, one dubious Jewish one—and the place of the eternal repose of a hero who is an inspiration to all mankind.

The Room of the Last Supper at Mount Zion.

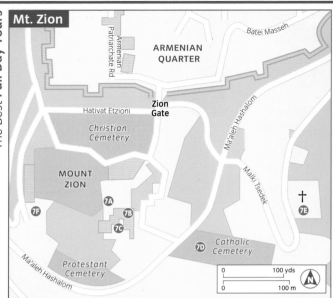

Mt. Zion

The **7A** ★★ **Room of the Last Supper (Coenaculum)** is believed to be where Jesus celebrated his last Passover Seder meal, with his disciples (open daily 8am–6pm). Below this Upper Room is **7B** **King David's Tomb,** venerated by some as the burial place of the monarch, although most scholars dispute this (open Sun–Thurs 8am–5:30pm; Fri, Sat & holidays 7:30am–2pm). Nearby is the **7C** **Chamber of the Holocaust,** a small, eerie private memorial to the Jewish victims of the Nazis (open Sun–Thurs 9am–3:45pm, Fri 9am–1:30pm; closed Sat). The **7D** ★ **Roman Catholic cemetery** on Mt. Zion is the final resting place of **Oskar Schindler,** the hero of *Schindler's List;* many come to pay tribute by placing a

small stone on his grave (open Mon–Sat 8am–2pm). The **7E** **Church of St. Peter in Gallicantu** marks the place where tradition holds that the disciple Peter disavowed Jesus three times before the cock crowed (open Mon–Sat 8:30am–5pm). Mt. Zion's most recognizable landmark is **7F** ★ **Haga Maria Sion (or Dormition) Abbey,** whose squat round tower is topped by a gray cone and four turrets. The Benedictine convent is so named because it is believed Mary fell into everlasting sleep here before her assumption into heaven. *Free admission to all sites. Dormition Abbey hours: Mon–Sat 8:30–11:45am; Mon–Fri 12:30–5pm, Sat 12:45–4:45pm; Sun 10:30–11:45am & 12:30–5pm.*

8 ★★ **The Citadel of David.** The citadel tower beside the Jaffa Gate is called the Tower of David, although historically this site was

developed 800 years after David died. Three massive towers built by Herod originally stood on this spot; each of the subsequent rulers of

Private Tour Guides

You may choose to hire a private guide to enjoy maximum flexibility and focus on exactly the places and topics you want to get to know better. The following are recommended English-speaking guides, licensed by the State of Israel, along with areas of expertise (although each is qualified in any area):

- **Honey Stollman:** Jerusalem, Dead Sea/Masada; ☎ 077/751-3412.
- **Suzanne Pomeranz:** Introductory full-day tour, ramparts, Christian sites, Ramat Rachel; ☎ 02/673-8192.
- **Hanitai Alyagon:** In the footsteps of Jesus, reconstructing the historic battles of ancient and modern Israel, the Templers; ☎ 052/422-6626.
- **Max Blackston:** Millennia of history in and around Jerusalem, Herodion; ☎ 02/567-1833.
- **Amir Cheshin:** The Old City, Jewish-Arab relations, in the footsteps of Mark Twain; ☎ 050/533-6027.
- **Shmuel Browns:** Underground Jerusalem (caverns and tunnels), Herodion; ☎ 02/561-0785.
- **Itamar Shapira:** Yad Vashem and the Old City from both a Palestinian and Israeli perspective; ☎ 054/808-7440.
- **Aram Khatchadourian:** An expert on the Armenian quarter; ☎ 050/335-1859.

Jerusalem—Romans, Byzantines, Mamluk Muslims, Crusaders, and Ottoman Turks—rebuilt these fortifications beside Jaffa Gate. The **Tower of David Museum of the History of Jerusalem** now occupies the citadel, which is a fascinating structure in and of itself, besides affording great views of the New and Old cities. ⏱ *1 hr.* ☎ *02/626-5333. www.towerofdavid.org.il. Admission NIS 30 adults; check for schedules of guided tours in English, included with admission. Sept–June Sun–Thurs 10am–4pm, Sat & holidays 10am–2pm, closed Fridays; July & August Sat–Thurs 10am–5pm, Fri 10am–2pm.*

⑨ ★★★ kids Israel Museum.
The Israel Museum boasts some of the most striking architecture in

The Israel Museum boasts several excellent collections.

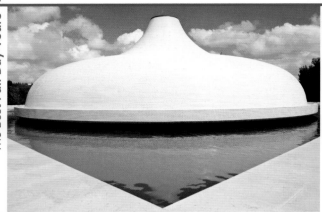

The Shrine of the Book is the home of the Dead Sea Scrolls.

West Jerusalem, but it is the museum's incredible collections that are the real attraction. The **Judaica Wing** houses the greatest artistic creations in the long history of the Jewish religion, gathered from the four corners of the earth. The **Archaeological Museum and Garden** contain ancient artifacts of almost unequalled historical importance, reflecting the antecedents, birth, and development of Judeo-Christian civilization. The **Billy Rose Art Garden** contains sculptures by Rodin (1840–1917), Picasso (1881–1973), and others, while the Floersheimer Pavilion for Impressionist and Post-Impressionist Art features works by Monet (1840–1926), Renoir—and other masters of the genres. The **Children's Wing** (see p 53) is dedicated to educating future generations about art and culture by means of entertaining interactive programs. ⏱ *1–2 hr. Ruppin St.* ☎ *02/670-8811. www. imj.org.il. Admission NIS 40 adults (dual- & multiple-entry tickets available). Sat–Mon, Wed & Thurs*
10am–5pm; Tues 4–9pm; Fri 10am–2pm. The box office is closed on Sat, but tickets may be purchased just outside the building from an authorized agent.

⓾ ★★★ The Shrine of the Book (Dead Sea Scrolls). Under the gleaming white parabolic roof, contoured to resemble the clay jars in which the Dead Sea Scrolls were discovered, resides the permanent home of the oldest known parchment documents in the Hebrew language. These scrolls, along with the Bar Kochba letters from the time of the Jews' revolt against Rome, are prized national and cultural treasures that are stored underground in case of enemy bombardment. The Shrine also contains finds from the legendary Dead Sea fortress of Masada; rare and priceless finds shedding light on ancient Israelite history are added to this exclusive collection from time to time. *Adjacent to the Israel Museum (see ⑨). Admission included with the Museum.*

Organized Tours

There are a number of tours available—some even free of charge—that can enhance any visit. The following private companies offer group tours of Jerusalem and nearby regions, led by licensed guides. Check the latest schedules and prices:

- **Zion Walking Tours** offers 3-hour tours of sections of the Old City, West Jerusalem, and even the Judean Desert. Located on Armenian Patriarchate Road (inside Jaffa Gate, opposite the police station next to the Tower of David). Call ☎ 02/627-7588 or visit http://zionwt.dsites1.co.il.
- **Egged Tours,** operated by the country's largest bus company, depart Jerusalem daily for tours of 1 to 3 days to all parts of Israel. Most hotel reception areas contain brochures with schedules, itineraries, and prices. Tours may be booked at travel agencies or travel desks at major hotels. Call ☎ 700/707-577 (or ☎ *3920) or visit www.eggedtours.com.
- An arm of **ICAHD (The Israeli Committee Against House Demolitions)** specializes in "alternative" tours from Palestinian, as well as Israeli, perspectives. Find it at the Travel Center at Damascus Gate, or call ☎ 054/693-4433 or check out www.toursinenglish.com.

The following group tours are free; while guides here are also very knowledgeable, they are not always licensed by the state:

- **Sandeman's Free Tours:** 3½-hour walking tours depart daily at 11am and 2:30pm from just outside the Jaffa Gate Tourist Information Office; look for staffers in red t-shirts. Call ☎ 02/624-4726 or visit www.newjerusalemtours.com. The guides work for tips; do not let yours go unrewarded.
- **Jerusalem Municipality:** Free walking tours in English are offered Saturdays at 10am from 32 Jaffa Rd. Call ☎ 02/531-4600.
- **The Society for the Protection of Nature in Israel:** Offers occasional free walking tours in English of Jerusalem neighborhoods. Call ☎ 02/625-2357.

For dinner, try the 🍴 ★★ **Armenian Tavern** in the Old City's Armenian Quarter. The best night is Friday, when the restaurant offers a special "Armenian kitchen" dish. Reservations are essential Friday and Saturday evenings. *79 Armenian Patriarchate Rd.* ☎ *02/627-3854. $$.*

The Best in **Three Days**

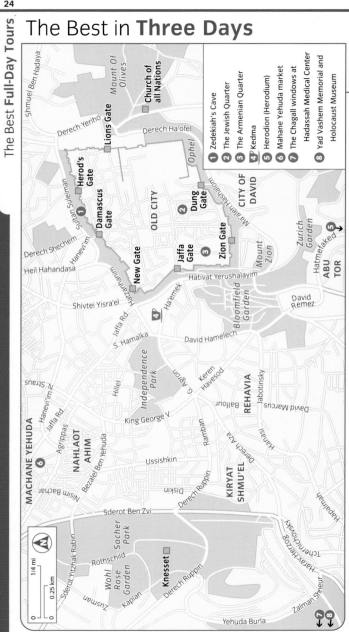

1 Zedekiah's Cave
2 The Jewish Quarter
3 The Armenian Quarter
4 Kedma
5 Herodion (Herodium)
6 Mahane Yehuda market
7 The Chagall windows at Hadassah Medical Center
8 Yad Vashem Memorial and Holocaust Museum

On the third day, we spread our wings a bit and travel outside the city—to the suburb of Ein Karem and the nearby Judean Desert. And we get acquainted with the outdoor Jewish market, with its colorful stalls of produce and ethnic foods, to the delight of our taste buds. START: **The Jewish Quarter, inside the Zion Gate.**

❶ ★ kids Zedekiah's Cave. This huge underground cavern, extending from the Old City Walls nearly all the way to the Temple Mount, reopened to the public in 2009. It is also known as Solomon's Quarries, since it is believed to be the quarry from which the stones for the ancient Temple were hewn. The cave is of special importance to the worldwide Order of Masons, which claims spiritual descent from the original builders of the First Temple. Jewish and Muslim legends claim that tunnels from here extended to the Sinai Desert and Jericho. The name comes from the story that King Zedekiah fled from the Babylonians through these tunnels in 587 BCE, only to be captured later near Jericho. An illuminated path leads you into this netherworld under the Old City. ⏱ *45 min. Entrance along the Old City Walls between Damascus Gate & Herod's Gate. ☎ 02/627-7550. Admission NIS 10 adults. Sun–Thurs 9am–5pm (9am–4pm in winter).*

❷ ★★ The Jewish Quarter of the Old City. By now, you will probably at least have passed through this area of the ancient city, which has been the center of the Jewish community in the Old City since 1267, when the Crusaders were driven from Jerusalem. The Jewish Quarter was destroyed by the Jordanians during and after Israel's War of Independence in 1948; since Israel retook the Old City in 1967, the quarter has been rebuilt and repopulated.

Zedekiah's Cave is a huge underground cavern underneath the Old City.

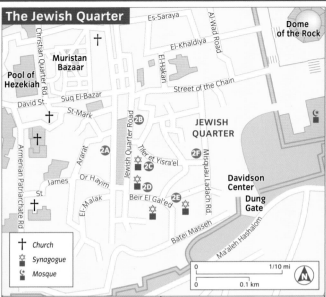

The Jewish Quarter

Es-Saraya

Al-Wad Road

Dome of the Rock

El-Khaldiya

Christian Quarter Rd.

Muristan Bazaar

El-Hakari

Pool of Hezekiah

David St.

Suq El-Bazar

Street of the Chain

St-Mark

Jewish Quarter Road

2B

JEWISH QUARTER

2A

Tif'er et Yisra'el

2F

2C

Misquau Ladach Rd.

Ararat

Or Hayim

2D

Davidson Center

James

Beir El Gal'ed

2E

Armenian Patriarchate Rd.

El Malak

Dung Gate

St

Batei Masseh

Ma'aleh Hashalom

† Church
☆ Synagogue
▪ Mosque

0   1/10 mi
0   0.1 km

The highlight of the Jewish Quarter is **2A ★★ the Cardo Maximus,** Jerusalem's main market street from the 2nd to 6th centuries (Roman and Byzantine times). The southern portion of the Cardo, with many original paving stones, is open to the sky and lined with imposing columns found and re-erected by archaeologists; note the walled-up facades of Crusader-era shops built into arches (some replaced by modern tourist shops). In this restored section, you can look down shafts that reveal how far above ancient street-level the city has risen after centuries of rebuilding on the ruins

of each wave of destruction. The massive **2B Broad Wall** was part of the city's defenses dating from the First Temple period (about 700 BCE). Other important sites in the Jewish Quarter are the **2C Hurva Synagogue,** now being rebuilt to its original striking dimensions, complete with a white dome that constitutes a new landmark in the panorama of the Old City; a complex of four small **2D Sephardic synagogues;** the **2E Wohl Archaeology Museum;** and the **2F Burnt House.** See p 35 for details on the Wohl Museum and Burnt House. ⏰ 1½ hr. www.jewish-quarter.org.il.

Travel Tip

The intricacies of the Armenian Quarter are difficult to explore on your own; visitors with a special interest in this community are advised to hire a specialized guide (see Private Tour Guides sidebar, p 21).

❸ ★ The Armenian Quarter.

Tucked between the Citadel of David and the Jewish Quarter is an area containing Armenian religious institutions dating back to the earliest centuries of Christianity. The Armenian Quarter does not yield its secrets easily: Access to the **Church**

St. James Cathedral in the Armenian Quarter.

of the Archangels—adjacent to the ★ **First Prison of Jesus,** as well as to the **Gulbenkian Library,** which houses some 4,000 illuminated manuscripts—is limited. The interior of the ★★ **St. James Cathedral** is one of the most interesting in the country, with chapels and altars richly adorned with ceramic tiles, mother of pearl, silver, and gold; dazzling chandeliers; dozens of hanging oil lamps; and a unique confessional. The church may be visited only during services (see p 42, ⑫, for schedule). The **Mardigian Museum of Armenian Art and History** contains a collection of artifacts and religious objects, and chronicles Armenian history. ☎ *02/628-2331. Admission to the museum NIS 5 adults. Mon–Sat 10am–4:30pm. The museum is closed for renovations for all of 2010.*

The Alrov Mamilla pedestrian mall that connects Jaffa Gate with the new city is Jerusalem's latest "coffee shop row." For the best variety—and most spectacular view—check out

Kedma, a meat restaurant (highlighting corned beef), coupled with a sister dairy restaurant (that features pasta). The beautiful coffee bar will not serve you milk, but the server will tell you where to obtain it for your coffee. *On the third floor of the interior mall.* ☎ *02/500-3737.$$. Kosher.*

⑤ ★★ **kids Herodion (Herodium).** Herodion is an oft-underrated site, partly because of its similarity to its more famous counterpart, Masada, and partly because it is a 25-minute drive from Jerusalem. For tourists who will not be visiting Masada, it is well worth the few hours it would take to visit the ruins of this cliff-top fortified palace that overlooks both Bethlehem and the Judean Desert, with views as far as the Dead Sea. (Tourists or pilgrims planning to visit Bethlehem can easily incorporate Herodion into this half-day excursion.) Herodion is so named because the magnificent tomb of the infamous monarch is here, alongside his winter palace and over-the-top swimming pool, which was kept filled for Herod's

Loaves of bread at the Mahane Yehuda market.

pleasure with water diverted from Jerusalem. The personality and paranoia of this notorious historical figure is reflected in the grandeur of the Herodion complex, complete with underground escape tunnels. ⏱ 1½ hr. (not including travel time). *Herodion is a national park on the edge of the Judean Desert.* ☎ *050/623-5821. www.parks.org.il. Admission NIS 25 adults; NIS 13 students, children & seniors. Sun–Thurs 8am–5pm, Fri 8am–2pm; closed Sat.*

⑥ ★★ The Chagall windows at Hadassah Medical Center. The largest medical center in the Middle East, the Hadassah-Hebrew University Medical Center stands on a hilltop several miles from downtown Jerusalem. The teaching hospital's synagogue is adorned by 12 exquisite stained-glass windows designed by renowned French-Jewish artist Marc Chagall (1887–1985). Each window depicts the Biblical blessing

(Gen. 49:1–27) that Jacob bestowed on his 12 sons destined to become the founders of the Twelve Tribes of Israel. Fans of Chagall will be happy to learn that more of his work—large, colorful tapestries—is on display in the Knesset (Parliament) building. ⏱ ½ hr. Ein Karem. ☎ *02/641-6333. Admission & tour of Chagall windows NIS 14 adults; discount for students & seniors. Sun–Thurs 8am–1:15pm & 2–3:45pm, Fri & eves of holidays 8am–12:30pm.*

⑦ ★★ kids Mahane Yehuda market. The open-air market—the *shook*—in West Jerusalem is very different from its counterpart in the Old City, but it is no less enjoyable. Israel's fruits and vegetables range from the familiar to the exotic; and like the breads, pastries, and cheeses you'll find here, all are at their freshest and tastiest at this bustling market. Along with the old-fashioned Jewish and ethnic foods on display, there are trendy cafes, sophisticated restaurants, healthful drinks, and even terrific ice cream. Taste the free samples (especially the halvah), shop for the best prices, and think about the terrific picnic for dinner or the next day's lunch you can provision here. And don't forget the wine. The market is at its busiest Thursdays and Fridays; prepare for slow going or to be jostled. It is closed Friday nights and Saturdays, although restaurants will reopen Saturday nights. Try to avoid Sunday, as many stalls are closed. ⏱ 1 hr. Opposite 110 Jaffa Rd. on the north side, or starting at 44 Agrippas St. on the south side; 5–10 minutes' walk west from downtown.

⑧ ★★★ Yad Vashem Memorial and Holocaust Museum. The world's largest institution dedicated to the commemoration of the Holocaust and its victims is located on the Ridge of Remembrance on Mt. Herzl, next to Israel's national military cemetery and the burial places of the leaders of the state of Israel.

Yad Vashem Memorial

Information

▪ *Point of Interest*

P *Parking*

🚻 *Rest Rooms*

Entry Gate

Hazikaron

0   100 yds
0   100 m

The Yad Vashem complex comprises the tunnel-shaped **8A Holocaust Museum,** wherein moving video testimonies by survivors are interspersed among exhibits that detail the suffering and near-extinction of European Jewry over the course of 12 years of Nazi persecution; the **8B Avenue of the Righteous Among the Nations,** lined with trees planted in honor of heroic gentiles (many of them martyred) who saved Jewish lives; the **8C Hall of Remembrance,** a crypt-like room where an eternal flame sheds somber light over plaques on the floor identifying dozens of death camps (the Hall's massive gate is unforgettable in and of itself); the **8D Hall of Names,** with the names, photographs, and personal details of as many of the victims as the institute has been able to gather; the 6m (20 ft.) **8E monument** to the 1.5 million Jewish soldiers among the Allied forces, partisans, and ghetto fighters; the **8F Valley of the Destroyed Communities,** memorializing 5,000 entire communities that were wiped off the face of the Earth; and the **8G Children of the Holocaust Memorial,** commemorating more than 1.5 million murdered children. ⏱ *2 hr. On Har Ha-Zikaron.* ☎ *02/675-1611. www. yadvashem.org.il. Free admission. Sun–Thurs 9am–4:45pm, Fri 9am–1pm; Hall of Names Sun–Thurs 10am–2pm, Fri 10am–1pm; archives & library Sun–Thurs 9am–3pm; all closed Sat & Jewish holidays.*

Visiting Yad Vashem

As difficult as the subject matter is, this is a uniquely enlightening, albeit depressing, experience for adults and teenaged children; parents should exercise discretion with regard to younger children. It is also an opportunity to sign a Remembrance Book that includes the comments and signatures of many world leaders. Visitors who do not feel they can complete the entire tour may wait for others in the new Art Museum, whose contents are less emotionally charged. *Warning:* It may be difficult for some to continue sightseeing as usual after a visit to Yad Vashem. If so, it is recommended to visit either during a rainy day or towards the end of the day, when all that is left to do is watch a golden sunset over the Eternal City. ●

Yad Vashem's Avenue of the Righteous Among the Nations.

2 The Best Special Interest Tours

Archaeology & History

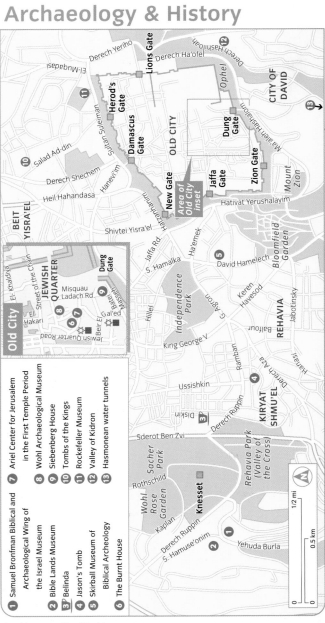

1. Samuel Bronfman Biblical and Archaeological Wing of the Israel Museum
2. Bible Lands Museum
3. Belinda
4. Jason's Tomb
5. Skirball Museum of Biblical Archeology
6. The Burnt House
7. Ariel Center for Jerusalem in the First Temple Period
8. Wohl Archaeological Museum
9. Siebenberg House
10. Tombs of the Kings
11. Rockefeller Museum
12. Valley of Kidron
13. Hasmonean water tunnels

Previous page: City of David.

Israel is a paradise for those who love to get a feel for history by looking at what our predecessors from antecedent cultures—Egyptians, Greeks, Romans, Crusaders, Ottomans—and religions left behind for us to discover. Since it has been a crossroads between Africa, Asia, and Europe for centuries, the country is dotted with archaeological sites. And as a city that has existed since Biblical times, Jerusalem has an incredible concentration of archeological excavations, as well as world-class museums where magnificent finds are on display. START: **Israel Museum, Ruppin Rd.**

1 ★★ **Samuel Bronfman Biblical and Archaeological Wing of the Israel Museum.** The largest collection anywhere of artifacts found in Israel is on display here, including stone and clay masks from Neolithic through early Canaanite periods; copper wands, scepters, crowns, and ceremonial maces from the Chalcolithic (Copper Age) sanctuary of a forgotten people (c. 3500 BCE); mosaic floors and architectural ornamentations from ancient Jewish and Samaritan synagogues; elaborate sarcophagi; and much more. There's a cafeteria available for snacks and drinks. ⏱ *2 hr. See p 21,* **9**.

2 ★★ kids **Bible Lands Museum.** This is another museum for art lovers, since objects of great beauty, as well as exquisitely designed ancient jewelry, are on display along with impressive

archaeological finds. The museum is arranged chronologically: Artifacts from differing cultures that existed at the same time are displayed side by side. Themes such as religious worship, trade, communication, and transportation are examined in ways that bring tremendous insight into ancient times. One particular bas-relief depiction of the life of Jesus is among the earliest known representations of Christ and elements of Christian theology. There is a cafeteria on the premises. ⏱ *2 hr. 25 Granot St., opposite the Israel Museum.* ☎ *02/561-1066. www.blmj.org. Admission NIS 32 adults; discounts for children, students & seniors. Sun–Tues & Thurs 9:30am–5:30pm, Wed 9:30am–9:30pm, Fri 9:30am–2pm; closed Sat & Jewish holidays. English-language tours offered daily 10:30am & Wed 5:30pm. Private tours may also be booked.*

A sculpture from the Israel Museum.

A woman examines an artifact from the Bible Lands museum.

A nice cafe on the edge of Rehavia is **3** ★ **Belinda** (see p 110). Before heading down the elevator, take in the panoramic view of the Knesset and Israel Museum. *9 Diskin St.* ☎ *02/563-3995. $$.*

4 **Jason's Tomb.** Exactly who Jason (mentioned in one of the several inscriptions here) was remains a mystery. What we do know is that he was an affluent Jerusalemite from the late Hasmonean period. Some think he was a priest identified in writings from that era; others believe he was a seafarer or

An excavation from The Burnt House.

merchant, since a wall drawing in the tomb depicts a ship with a man standing on its deck. The tomb is located in the present-day affluent residential neighborhood of Rehavia, which was probably built over a burial complex from the Second Temple period. The structure (especially the pyramid-shaped top) recalls Zachariah's Tomb in the Kidron Valley (See p 91, **1**). ⏱ *15 min. 10 Alfasi St. No phone. Free admission.*

5 ★ **Skirball Museum of Biblical Archeology.** Appended to the Israel campus of the seminary for Reform Jewish rabbis is this modern museum housing a collection of objects discovered in good part from Tel Dan in the north. If you're with people not as keen about archaeology as you are, there are good English periodicals in the adjacent library. ⏱ *45 min. Hebrew Union College, 13 King David St.* ☎ *02/620-3333. Free admission. Sun–Thurs 10am–4pm, Sat 10am–2pm.*

6 **The Burnt House.** This discovery chillingly recalls the day in 70 CE when the Romans burned Jerusalem's Upper City. Archaeologists found here the forearm bones of a young woman, as well as a wooden spear and a set of weights marked with the name "Bar Kathros," a

The Case of the Silver Scrolls

One of Israel's most amazing archaeological finds was discovered in 1979, when two tiny silver scrolls inscribed with the priestly blessing (Numbers 6:23) were found in an ancient burial chamber. Now on display at the Israel Museum, these antique amulets represent the oldest surviving remnants of texts from the Hebrew Bible, dating back to approximately 600 BCE. If you want to view the excavation where the scrolls were found, the best vantage point is from the landing of the stairs leading up to St. Andrews Church (1 David Remez St.).

priestly family responsible for the manufacture of incense for the Temple. A brief slide show explains the finds at the site. ⏱ *30 min. 13 Tiferet Israel St.* ☎ *02/628-7211. Admission NIS 14 adults; NIS 26 adults combined ticket with the Wohl Museum (see below). Sun–Thurs 9am–5pm, Fri 9am–noon.*

❼ Ariel Center for Jerusalem in the First Temple Period.

The permanent exhibition of this Old City branch of the Yad Ben Zvi's institute for the study of Jerusalem contains archeological findings and models that demonstrate daily life in Jerusalem from the time of King David to the period of the Assyrian

siege and its surprising failure. ⏱ *20 min. Bonei Hahomah St., corner of Plugat Hakotel St.* ☎ *02/628-6288. Admission NIS 18 adults, NIS 14 students & seniors. Sun–Thurs 9am–4pm, Fri 9am–1pm.*

❽ ★ Wohl Archaeological Museum—Herodian Quarter.

The Wohl Museum contains finds from the wealthy residential quarter of Herodian Jerusalem, including remains of a palatial mansion with painted faux marble walls, mosaic floors, an atrium pool, and ritual baths. ⏱ *45 min. 1 Karaim St.* ☎ *02/626-5922. Admission NIS 14 adults; NIS 26 adults combined ticket with the Burnt House (see*

Inside the Wohl Archaeological Museum.

The entrance to the Tombs of the Kings.

above). *Sun–Thurs 9am–5pm, Fri 9am–1pm.*

❾ ★ Siebenberg House. Excavations beneath the Siebenberg home have revealed remains of dwellings, aqueducts, and burial vaults, as well as rare artifacts dating back to the times of King Solomon and the Second Temple period. There are guided tours and a slide show. *⏱ 30 min. 5 Beit Hasho'eva Alley (lower part of Batei-Mahse Rd.), Jewish Quarter. ☎ 054/726-7754. Admission NIS 20 adults. Sun–Thurs 9:30am–6pm.*

❿ ★ Tombs of the Kings. A gate marked Tombeau des Rois leads down to a hollowed-out courtyard with several small cave openings; one of them contains four sarcophagi decorated with carvings of fruit and vines. The name is not quite precise, since no kings are buried here; but the tomb was indeed royal: the family of Queen Helena of the Mesopotamian province of Adiabene, who converted to Judaism in Jerusalem around 50 CE. *⏱ 30 min. Behind St. George's on Saladin St. Admission NIS 5 adults. Mon–Sat 8am–12:30pm & 2–5pm.*

⓫ ★★ Rockefeller Museum. This edifice, an eclectic design that combines elements of Byzantine, Islamic, and Art Deco styles, is probably the most significant secular landmark in East Jerusalem. It was built in 1927 courtesy of a $2 million gift from U.S. philanthropist John D. Rockefeller (1839–1937). Now a branch of the Israel Museum, the building houses regional archaeological finds ranging from the Stone Age to the 18th century, including bas-relief stonework that once

Archaeologist for the Day

Amateur archaeologists of all ages (children are welcome) can get their chance to "dig for a day" at an honest-to-goodness archaeological site. Two organizations that will be happy to arrange such a field trip for you are **City of David** (☎ *6033) and **Archaeological Seminars** (☎ 02/586-2011; www.archesem.com).

adorned the entrance to the Church of the Holy Sepulcher, the 9th-century carved wooden panels and ceiling beams of the Al Aqsa Mosque, and elaborate Islamic motifs from the 8th-century Palace of Hisham near Jericho. There is also a gallery of Egyptian antiquities, and a Paleolithic section contains the bones of a pre-historic Homo sapien dubbed Mount Carmel Man; the skeletal remains were found in the hills near Haifa. Enjoy also the museum's cloister garden set around a reflecting pool. Always inquire about closures due to renovation. ⏱ *1½ hr. 27 Sultan Suleiman St., opposite Herod's Gate. ☎ 02/628-2251. www.english.imjnet.org.il. Free admission. Sun, Mon, Wed & Thurs 10am–3pm; Sat 10am–2pm; closed Tues & Fri.*

⑫ ★★ Valley of Kidron. Ancient burial caves line the valley now occupied by the Arab village of Silwan, where residents and their ancestors have incorporated the caves right into their dwellings. The most outstanding tombs are the **Tomb of [the Prophet] Zechariah,** a cube-shaped structure crowned by a 40-foot high pyramid; **The Tomb of the Sons of Hezir,** a priestly family mentioned in the Bible (the columned entrance is hewn right into the rock); and **Absalom's Tomb,** ascribed to Absalom, the son of King David who rebelled against his father. Whether it dates back that far or not, scholars agree it goes back at least to Herodian times—making it Jerusalem's only relatively intact structure from before the Roman destruction in 70 CE. ⏱ *30 min. See p 19,* ⑤.

⑬ ★★ kids Hasmonean water tunnels. Underneath the present-day Goldman Promenade (and what is known to Christians as the Hill of Evil Counsel) winds an incredible system that carried water in Judean Kingdom times from beyond Bethlehem to Jerusalem to link up with Hezekiah's Tunnel. Visitors can walk through a sizable stretch of the underground channel, which is completely dry these days. Visit these tunnels only with a guide, either a private one (see p 21) or one through the City of David organization. ⏱ *2 hr. ☎ *6033. http://city ofdavid.org.il. Free admission.*

The excavated Tomb of Zechariah.

Jerusalem Religious Sites

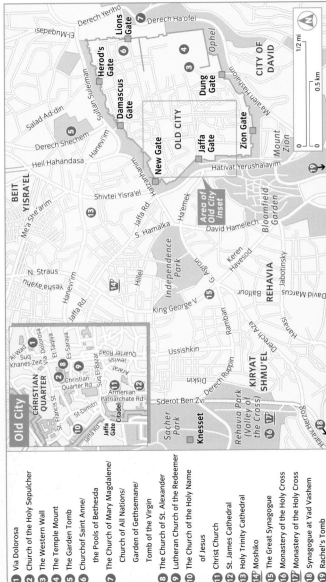

Old City

CHRISTIAN QUARTER

JEWISH QUARTER

ARMENIAN QUARTER

Al-Wad
Suq
Khanes-Zeit
El-Tadya
Via Dolorosa
Es-Saraya
Suq El-Bazar
Christian Quarter Rd.
St-Francis St.
St-Dimitri
Jaffa Rd
Jaffa Gate
Citadel
Ararat
Armenian Patriarchate Rd

Derech Yeriho
Derech Ha'ofel
Lions Gate
El-Mugadasi
Herod's Gate
Damascus Gate
Sultan Suleiman
Ophel
CITY OF DAVID
Dung Gate
Salad Ad-din
Ma'aleh Hashalom
Derech Shechem
Hanevi'im
New Gate
OLD CITY
Jaffa Gate
Zion Gate
Mount Zion
Heil Hahandasa
Hatzanhanim
Mea She'arim
Shivtei Yisra'el
Hativat Yerushalayim
BEIT YISRA'EL
Jaffa Rd.
S. Hamalka
Ha'emek
Area of Old City inset
David Hamelech
Bloomfield Garden
N. Straus
Hanevi'im
Yesha'ayahu
Independence Park
Keren Hayesod
Jabotinsky
Hillel
G. Agron
King George V
Ramban
REHAVIA
Balfour
David Marcus
Ussishkin
Aza
Derech Aza
Hanasi
Sacher Park
Knesset
Diskin
Derech Ruppin
KIRYAT SHMU'EL
Sderot Ben-Zvi
Rehavia Park (Valley of the Cross)
Hatzvi Herzog

Wile other cities in the world may also claim to be sacred to one specific religion or another, only Jerusalem may be considered undisputedly holy to all three of the Western world's monotheistic religions. This tour includes some of the venerated sites featured in Chapter 1 and adds yet more places of particular interest to Jewish and Christian visitors. START: **Antonia's Fortress near Lion's Gate.**

Travel tip

Some of the other major Jewish, Christian, and Muslim religious sites have been reviewed in Chapter 1.

❶ ★★★ **Via Dolorosa.** The Sanctuaries of the Flagellation and the Condemnation, where Jesus was scourged and judged, represent the first Station of the Cross (opposite Ecce Homo Basilica). The other Stations are (2) Jesus receives the cross; (3) Jesus falls for the first time (now the site of a biblical archaeology museum); (4) Jesus sees his mother; (5) Simon the Cyrene helps Jesus carry the cross; (6) Veronica wipes Jesus's face, and his visage is imprinted on the fabric; (7) Jesus falls the second time; (8) Jesus consoles the women of Jerusalem; (9) Jesus falls the third time (presently the Coptic Monastery). The five remaining Stations of the Cross are inside the Church of the Holy Sepulcher (see below, bullet ❷): (10) Jesus is stripped of his garments; (11) Jesus is nailed to the cross; (12) Jesus dies on the cross; (13) Jesus is taken down from the cross and given to Mary; (14) Jesus is laid in the chamber of the sepulcher and from there is resurrected. ⏱ *1 hr. Station One is at Antonia's Fortress, not far from Lions' Gate. Open daily 8am–noon; Apr–Sept 2–6pm, Oct–Mar 1–5pm. See p 12,* ❺.

❷ ★★★ **Church of the Holy Sepulcher.** The church, located on the site of the tomb from which it is believed Jesus rose, was first built by the Roman Emperor Constantine in 326 CE. Fire, earthquake, Persian conquerors (who carried off remnants of the Holy Cross in the 7th century), and an 11th-century Muslim caliph destroyed much of the classical church; the Crusaders rebuilt it in the 12th century in medieval Frankish style, while preserving Byzantine remnants. *See p 12,* ❻.

❸ ★★★ **The Western Wall.** ⏱ *1 hr. See p 9.*

❹ ★★★ **The Temple Mount.** ⏱ *30 min. See p 10.*

❺ ★★ **The Garden Tomb.** This 1st-century tomb is believed by some to be the tomb of Jesus. After it was discovered in 1867 by Dr. Conrad Schick (1822–1901), British General C. G. Gordon (1833–1885) visited the tomb in 1883 and—after spying a nearby hill that looked like a skull, which he identified as Golgotha (Calvary) or the New Testament's "Place of the Skull"—declared it the real tomb of Jesus. It was found, after its excavation in 1891, to meet some

The detailed tile work of Al Aqsa Mosque.

Weekly Drama along the Via Dolorosa

Let the Franciscan monks be your guides to the stations of the Via Dolorosa. Every Friday afternoon at 4pm, a group of monks sets out from the Antonia Fortress (Station One) and proceeds along the entire route, explaining the event at each station over a portable loudspeaker in Italian and English. There is continuous praying and chanting along the way, by the monks, pilgrims, and tourists. The confluence of the three religions is lived out as the Muslim call to prayer will also be sounded at some point during the procession. In the winter season, when the sun sets early, soon after the procession ends, Jews will be dancing down to the Western Wall to welcome the Sabbath.

of the criteria: close to the site of the crucifixion, outside the walls of the city, a tomb hewn from rock for a rich man, and situated in a garden. It is maintained by Protestant volunteers from the U.K. 🕐 *30 min. Conrad Schick St., off Nablus Rd. opposite Damascus Gate.* ☎ *02/628-3402. Free admission (donations accepted). Mon–Sat 8am–12:15pm & 2:30–5:15pm. Protestant service in English Sun 9am.*

❻ ★ Church of Saint Anne and the Pools of Bethesda.

This exquisite 12th-century Crusader church, erected in honor of the birthplace of Mary, the mother

The Church of Mary Magdalene on the Mount of Olives.

of Jesus (and thus named in honor of Mary's mother, Anne), was built next to the double-pool of Bethesda, the site where Jesus is believed to have performed healing miracles. An underground crypt contains a rock-hewn altar where Franciscans have been reciting mass since the 16th century. The church's acoustics are renowned: Pilgrim groups come to sing here throughout the day; any visitor is free to sing a song or hymn of any religion. 🕐 *30 min. Just inside Lion's Gate (St. Stephen's Gate). Admission NIS 10 adults. Mon–Sat 8am–noon & 2–5pm (until 6pm in summer); closed Sun.*

❼ ★★ The Church of Mary Magdalene/Church of All Nations/Garden of Gethsemane/Tomb of the Virgin.

Some of the leading Christian holy sites in Jerusalem are located at the foot of the Mt. of Olives, below the eastern walls of the Old City. The sites are both outdoors and indoors. 🕐 *1 hr. See p 92,* ❻.

❽ ★★ The Church of St. Alexander. Portraits of the last Romanovs still hang inside this Russian Orthodox church built in 1896.

The ceiling of The Church of the Holy Name of Jesus.

Ring the bell for entry and walk down the stairs to an arch that rests on two capitals and a pillar. The 2nd-century arch was part of a triumphal gate to the Forum, built by the Emperor Hadrian (76–138). The threshold, under glass, is thought by some to be the Judgment Gate through which Jesus passed on his way to Golgotha. ⏲ *30 min. Off Muristan Rd.* ☎ *02/627-4952. Free admission. Tues–Sun 9am–6pm.*

⑨ ★ Lutheran Church of the Redeemer. Kaiser Wilhelm II (1859–1941) of Germany made a pilgrimage to the Holy Land in 1898 to dedicate the Church of the Redeemer, a Protestant church built as close as was possible to the Church of the Holy Sepulcher, on the site of a 12th-century Crusader Knights of St. John hostel named St. Mary Latin Minor. Turkish permission to allow construction of a Protestant church at such a prestigious location symbolized the growing alliance between Germany and the Ottoman Empire, one that would continue through World War I. The church has become a venue for concerts and organ music performances; the view from the tower (no elevator, and a steep climb of more than 200 steps) is exceptional. ⏲ *30 min. Between Muristan Bazaar*

& Suq Khan ez-Zeit Bazaar. ☎ *02/627-6111. Admission to tower NIS 5 adults. Mon–Sat 9am–1pm & 2–5pm. English services in restored 12th-century chapel Sun 9am.*

⑩ The Church of the Holy Name of Jesus. Also known as the co-Cathedral of the Diocese of Jerusalem, it was consecrated in 1872 as the "mother" church of the Latin Patriarchate of Jerusalem, the official name of the Roman Catholic Diocese that was established here in 1847. The interior is much like walking into a miniature of a

Inside the Church of St. Alexander.

cathedral in France. ⏱ *20 min. Latin Patriarchate Rd.* ☎ *02/628-2323. Free admission. Daily 7am–7pm.*

⑪ ★ Christ Church. The first Protestant Church to be built in Jerusalem (in 1838) was built to resemble a synagogue so that neighboring Jews would feel comfortable—and perhaps be persuaded to convert. Its stained glass windows portray both Jewish and Christian symbols. A helpful American-born volunteer is often on hand to explain the history of the church. ⏱ *30 min. Opposite the Citadel of David. Open daily.*

⑫ ★★ St. James Cathedral. The primary house of worship for the Armenian Orthodox Patriarchate dates from the 11th century and is built on the site of even earlier churches. If you arrive on time for the service, you can witness a novice priest summoning worshipers to prayer by knocking on a wooden bar, as well as older priests with black cowls arriving. Be sure to stay for the chanting. The sanctuary contains a large antique globe that is unfortunately mostly hidden. Just inside the entrance are informational pamphlets about the Armenian Patriarchate and community. ⏱ *45 min. Entry through the Armenian Monastery on Armenian Patriarchate Rd. Services (the only times tourists are permitted to visit) Sun–Fri 6:30–7:30am & 3–3:30 pm, Sat 6:30–9:30am.*

⑬ ★ Holy Trinity Cathedral. This immense Russian Orthodox church, reminiscent of the Church of the Ascension in the Kremlin, was the first Christian house of worship to be built outside the Old City, in the mid-19th century. With exterior walls of almost alabaster white and numerous onion domes, it is one of those rare churches whose outside rivals the inside. ⏱ *15 min. Russian Compound,*

Heleni Hamalka St. ☎ *02/625-2525. Mon–Sat 9am–1pm.*

⑭ Moshiko is a centrally located shwarma joint that offers an incredible array of salads to be stuffed with your meat into a pita. No extra charge for the vegetables or condiments; if you want a large selection, opt for the larger lafa (wrap) option—and grab plenty of napkins. It's open 'til midnight, making it a great place for a late-night snack. *5 Ben Yehuda St. (the pedestrian mall). No phone. $.*

⑮ The Great Synagogue. Jerusalem's Great Synagogue is twinned with Heichal Shlomo, the domed building that houses the headquarters of Israel's Chief Rabbinate. The sanctuary's stained glass windows are among the most beautiful and majestic in the country. It is the only synagogue in the country with a full-time choirmaster and professional choir; services on major Jewish holidays attract both worshipers and lovers of cantorial music. ⏱ *30 min. 56 King George St.* ☎ *02/623-0628. www.jerusalemgreatsynagogue. com. Daily until noon.*

⑯ ★★ Monastery of the Holy Cross. This venerable Greek Orthodox monastery is one of the underappreciated sites of Jerusalem. It was built on the ruins of a 5th-century church erected on the place where tradition holds the tree grew that was used to make Christ's cross. The outside resembles a fortress, since it lacked the protection of the city walls; once inside, it is easy to forget this is a monastery: there is a charming, albeit sparse, garden with cages of parakeets; an exhibit of ancient maps, a centuries-old kitchen that has been preserved—and scarcely a monk in

One of the beautiful stained glass windows from The Great Synagogue.

sight. The chapel is a jewel, with a mosaic that dates back to the 11th century. 🕐 *45 min. Valley of the Cross.* ☎ *052/221-5144. Admission NIS 2 adults. Mon–Sat 8:30am–6pm.*

The refreshment area in the aforementioned garden of the **17** Monastery of the Holy Cross is a pleasant place to sip a cold drink, have a cup of coffee, or cool off with an ice cream. *$.*

A mosaic from the Monastery of the Holy Cross.

18 ★ **Synagogue at Yad Vashem**. This is a chapel that doubles as a museum showcasing Judaica from destroyed synagogues in Europe. The new synagogue, designed by architect Moshe Safdie (see Three Architects Who Transformed Jerusalem, p 48), serves as both a house of prayer and a monument to the synagogues of Europe that no longer exist. Among the 31 items on display are four Torah arks from Romania and other Judaica from throughout Europe. *Mount of Remembrance. Free admission. Sun–Thurs 9am–5pm, Fri 9am–2pm.*

19 **Rachel's Tomb.** The burial place of the matriarch Rachel, wife of Jacob, is located at the entrance to Bethlehem, right on the border of Israel and the Palestinian Authority. It is visited mostly by Orthodox Jews, especially women who go there to pray for fertility, as Rachel did in the book of Genesis before giving birth to Joseph. 🕐 *15 min. The Jerusalem-Bethlehem Road. No phone. Open daily; it is not recommended to visit after dark or on the Jewish Sabbath.*

Architectural Landmarks

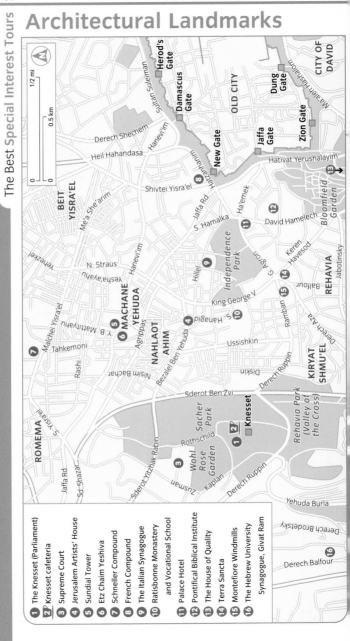

0   1/2 mi

0   0.5 km

Herod's Gate

Damascus Gate

New Gate

Jaffa Gate

Zion Gate

Dung Gate

OLD CITY

CITY OF DAVID

Ma'aleh HaShalom

Sultan Suleiman

Derech Shechem

Heil Hahandasa

Shivtei Yisra'el

Hativat Yerushalayim

Bloomfield Garden

BEIT YISRA'EL

Me'a She'arim

Jaffa Rd.

Ha'emek

David Hamelech

Haneviim

HaZanhanim

S. Hamalka

⑪

⑫

⑬

N. Straus

Yesha'ayahu

Hanevi'im

Hillel

Independence Park

Keren Hayesod

REHAVIA

Jabotinsky

Yehezkel

Malchei Yisra'el

MACHANE YEHUDA

Y. B. Mattityahu

⑤

King George V

S. Hanagid

G. Agron

Balfour

Ramban

⑨

⑩

⑭

⑮

Tahkemoni

⑦

Rashi

Agrippas

NAHLAOT AHIM

Bezalel Ben Yehuda

Nisim Bachar

④

Ussishkin

Diskin

Derech Ruppin

KIRYAT SHMU'EL

Derech Aza

S. Yisra'el

ROMEMA

Sderot Ben-Zvi

Jaffa Rd.

Sd. Shazar

Sderot Yitzhak Rabin

Zusman

Rothschild

Sacher Park

Wohl Rose Garden

Kaplan

Knesset

① ②

Rehavia Park (Valley of the Cross)

Derech Ruppin

Yehuda Burla

Derech Brodetsky

Derech Balfour

⑯

① The Knesset (Parliament)
②′ Knesset cafeteria
③ Supreme Court
④ Jerusalem Artists' House
⑤ Sundial Tower
⑥ Etz Chaim Yeshiva
⑦ Schneller Compound
⑧ French Compound
⑨ The Italian Synagogue
⑩ Ratisbonne Monastery and Vocational School
⑪ Palace Hotel
⑫ Pontifical Biblical Institute
⑬ The House of Quality
⑭ Terra Sancta
⑮ Montefiore Windmills
⑯ The Hebrew University Synagogue, Givat Ram

The many cultural influences that have left their mark on Jerusalem over the centuries are reflected in a number of remarkable buildings. European governments and churches built hospitals and compounds for their communities of residents and pilgrims; wealthy Arabs lived in stunning villas. It is only in recent years that places have begun to be marked for preservation; many were torn down, while others continue to deteriorate. Look for the trilingual blue plaques on the buildings, which explain those buildings' origins. START: **The Knesset, Kiryat Ben-Gurion.**

1 ★★★ The Knesset (Parliament). The current seat of Israel's legislature was constructed in the 1960s and donated as a gift to the Jewish state by James A. de Rothschild (1878–1957). The massive gate is the work of sculptor David Palombo (1920–1966), who also fashioned the dramatic doors at Yad Vashem. Just opposite the entryway is a small enclosure containing the Knesset Menorah, a gift from the British Parliament in 1956. Modeled after the menorah represented in the Arch of Titus, it depicts events and symbols of Jewish history. The Knesset interior is also worth a visit to view the large and colorful Chagall tapestries. Security is tight (you must show your passport) and there is a dress code officially (if not always in practice) barring shorts, jeans, and sandals without socks for men. ⏱ *30 min. Government Complex (Kiryat Ben-Gurion).*

☎ *02/675-3333. www.knesset.gov. il. Free admission and free guided tours Sun & Thurs 8:30am–2:30pm; viewing of Knesset sessions Mon & Thurs 4–9pm, Wed after 11am–end of session.*

The **2 Knesset cafeteria** is open to parliamentarians and visitors alike, so here is a chance to get up close and personal with Israeli politicians, who are generally quite approachable. The self-service cafeteria often features dishes representing considerable ethnic variety. *$$.*

3 ★★ Supreme Court. Only 18 years old, this impressive building is a must for modern architecture enthusiasts. The contemporary design incorporates Middle Eastern motifs of domes, arches, and passageways that create interesting interplays of shadow and light. Be

Inside The Knesset, the Israeli legislature.

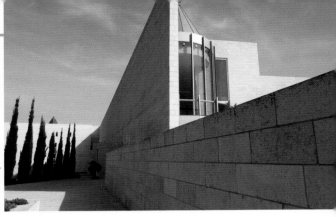

The modern Israeli Supreme Court building.

prepared for security inspections similar to those at the Knesset (see above). ⏱ *1 hr. Government Complex, next to Knesset.* ☎ *02/675-9612. Sun–Thurs 8:30am–2:30pm; free tours in English Sun–Thurs at noon.*

❹ ★ Jerusalem Artists' House. Today known as Artists' House, a venue for exhibits and cultural events, this three-story Ottoman Turkish building briefly served as Israel's national museum, right after independence. For decades, it was the home of the Bezalel School of Art, the country's foremost art institute (since moved to the campus of the Hebrew University on Mt. Scopus). *See p 86. 12 Shmuel HaNagid St.*

❺ ★ Sundial Tower. The Tiferet Zion Veyerushalayim Hostel was built by an American rabbi in 1908. One floor housed the Zoharei Hama (Rays of the Sun) Synagogue, while a system of clocks was installed on the third floor, centering around a unique aerial sundial—accurate to within 15 minutes. *92 Jaffa Rd.*

❻ Etz Chaim Yeshiva. Not only is the seminary building itself noteworthy for its size and pinkish stone, the detached facade extends for several blocks. When the light rail begins running, the sleek, modern tram will glide futuristically past the lovely 19th-century fronting. *113–115 Jaffa Rd.*

Jerusalem Stone

As you walk around the city, you will note the near uniformity of building exteriors, whether commercial properties or residences. This is because there is a city ordinance, dating back to British Mandatory Palestine (1917-1948), requiring all edifices to have stone facing, in order to maintain the durability and uniqueness of the Eternal City. "Jerusalem stone," as it is called, has become a popular motif in other Israeli cities, as well—and, on a smaller scale, in Judaica art objects.

7 Schneller Compound. This sprawling compound was designed by Conrad Schick (see sidebar) and served during the early 20th century as an orphanage. It is now mostly off-limits as a medical facility for the Israel Defense Forces. *46–48 Malkhei Yisrael St.*

8 ★★★ French Compound. In the second half of the 19th century, several European powers entered into an unofficial competition over who would have the most impressive physical presence in the Holy City. It is no wonder, therefore, that some of the city's most beautiful buildings are the Italian Hospital (p 74), Sergei Courtyard in the Russian Compound (p 59), and the two buildings comprising the French Compound: St. Louis Hospital and Notre Dame right next door. The Notre Dame de France, built in 1881, is a majestic symmetrical edifice topped by a statue of the Madonna holding the infant Jesus aloft. It is now known as the Pontifical Institute of Notre Dame, since ownership of the property was ceded to the Vatican. Diagonally across the street from the hospital is the church associated with the compound, the Convent Church of St. Vincent de Paul, now

The unique aerial sundial of the Sundial Tower.

the lovely centerpiece of the Alrov Mamilla Blvd. mall. *Corner of Hativat Hatzanhanim & Shivtei Yisrael sts.*

9 ★ The Italian Synagogue. This building, built in 1887 as a Christian girls' school in neo-Gothic style with pointed arches, now has one of the most exquisite interiors in all of Jerusalem: The entire sanctuary of the 18th-century synagogue of Conegliano (near Venice), Italy, was transposed here and now serves the local Italian Jewish community. Another part of the building

The entrance to the Artists' House.

Three Architects Who Transformed Jerusalem

Two European architects active in Jerusalem in the previous century made some of the most significant contributions to the city's landscape. **Antonio Barluzzi** (1884–1960), a Roman native, came to Jerusalem in 1917 and subsequently became the chief architect working under the direction of the Franciscan Order—the custodians of all papal property in the Holy Land. In this capacity, he designed some of the most important churches in the Galilee and Jerusalem, including the Church of all Nations in Gethsemane, Dominus Flevit on the Mt. of Olives, and the Church of the Visitation in Ein Karem. Unlike Barluzzi, **Conrad Schick** was not a trained architect; yet this did not prevent him from designing some of Jerusalem's most notable buildings, including the German Hospital, Talitha Kumi, and the neighborhood of Mea Shearim. Contemporary Israeli architect **Moshe Safdie** (1938–) has been a guiding force behind the Yad Vashem Memorial Complex and the rebuilding of the Jewish Quarter and Mamilla.

is an Italian Jewish museum (see p 127). It is possible to view the synagogue without entering the museum. ⏱ *15 min. 27 Hillel St.*

⑩ ★★ Ratisbonne Monastery and Vocational School. Established in 1874 by Alfred Ratisbonne, this is arguably the most beautiful monastery in Jerusalem. The building, a combination of Italian Renaissance and Romanesque styles, is occupied by a French Salesian order, les Pères de Sion. Next door, the curved edifice on the corner of King George Street is the large Yeshurun Synagogue, once Jerusalem's central synagogue; it has recently been twinned with the Bet Avi Hai Cultural Center. A walk through the monastery's driveway and parking lot leads to a pleasant plaza shared with a luxury condominium building. *26 Shmuel HaNagid St. No admission beyond the parking area.*

⑪ ★★ Palace Hotel. Once the most elegant hotel in Jerusalem, what is left now is its magnificent facade, being meticulously incorporated into a luxury condominium project being built by Waldorf-Astoria. Across Agron Street, at the foot of Independence Park, is a centuries-old Muslim cemetery containing many intact gravestones. *King David St., at the corner of Agron.*

⑫ ★ Pontifical Biblical Institute. Not to be confused with the Pontifical Institute of Notre Dame (see p 47, ⑧), this handsome building next to the French consulate was built in 1926, in an eclectic style with Renaissance elements. *3 Emile Botta St.* ☎ *02/625-2843.*

⑬ ★ The House of Quality. Once part of an ophthalmic hospital (dealing with diseases and surgery of the visual pathways) built at the turn of the 20th century by the

The Ratisbonne Monastery is a combination of Italian Renaissance and Romanesque styles.

Scottish Order of St. John, with the help of other orders—all of whose coats of arms can be seen on this building and the (even nicer, but less accessible) one directly across the street. The House of Quality is now an artists' cooperative and gallery of the elite of Jerusalem's artisans (see p 88). Check out also the Armenian tile room. (The building opposite contains the remains of a primitive cable car that ferried supplies and sustained the residents of the Old City's Jewish Quarter during Israel's War of Independence.)
🕐 *15 min. 12 Hebron Rd.*

⑭ Terra Sancta. This monumental ecclesiastical structure, designed by Antonio Barluzzi (see sidebar), combines Italian Renaissance and neo-baroque elements. A member of Italy's royal family came to Jerusalem in 1928 to dedicate the statue of the haloed Madonina, patron saint of Milano, on the roof. *France Sq., Keren Hayesod St.*

⑮ ★ Montefiore Windmills. One of the two stone windmills built in the 1870s has been cleverly incorporated into a small, lovely, upscale commercial complex in the neighborhood of Rechavia, very close to downtown. The other is in Yemin Moshe (p 65, ❸). *8 Ramban St.*

⑯ ★ The Hebrew University Synagogue, Givat Ram. This unique chapel might remind some of a button mushroom, but it was designed in the shape of a *kippah* (yarmulke, or skullcap). *Student housing, Givat Ram Campus.*

The Montefiore Windmill, built in the 1870s.

Jerusalem with Kids

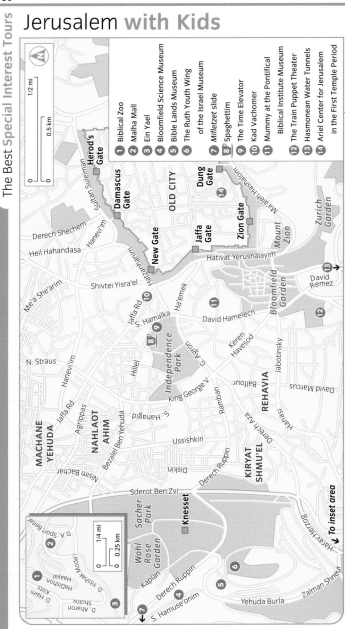

1 Biblical Zoo
2 Malha Mall
3 Ein Yael
4 Bloomfield Science Museum
5 Bible Lands Museum
6 The Ruth Youth Wing of the Israel Museum
7 *Mifletzet* slide
8 *Spaghettim*
9 The Time Elevator
10 Kad Vachomer
11 Mummy at the Pontifical Biblical Institute Museum
12 The Train Puppet Theater
13 Hasmonean Water Tunnels
14 Ariel Center for Jerusalem in the First Temple Period

Jerusalem is a city that is home to tens of thousands of families with young children, so activities abound, indoors and out; moreover, many are free or very reasonably priced. During school vacations (particularly in summer and during the Jewish holidays of Hanukkah, Passover, and Sukkot), most museums and cultural institutions offer special activities. START: **The Biblical Zoo, near the Malha Railway Station.**

1 ★★ Biblical Zoo. The emphasis of the Tisch Family Zoological Gardens is on creatures mentioned in the Bible or native to Israel, but it also houses many animals from countries near and far. Children will especially enjoy the friendly waterfowl, the miniature train, and the camel and pony rides. In the heat of a summer day, many of the animals are inactive; the zoo is at its best when it cools down. The zoo includes multiple refreshment stands. ⏱ *2 hr. Manahat.* ☎ *02/675-0111. www.jerusalemzoo.org.il. Admission NIS 42 adults, NIS 34 children. Sat–Thurs 9am–6pm (until 5pm in winter); Fri 9am–4pm. Admission ends an hour before closing time.*

2 Malha Mall. It may seem like just an ordinary shopping mall, but this is a good place to take kids on a rainy day or on a scorcher, when prolonged exposure to air-conditioning is called for. There is often children's entertainment, and fun animals and parrots on display. The two-level, all-kosher food court has all kinds of familiar and unfamiliar food in a non-threatening environment that will encourage picky eaters to become a bit more adventurous. Or combat homesickness at Burger King, KFC, or Pizza Hut (not in the food court, but also kosher). Parents will find extraordinary shopping here, and Wi-Fi access. *Malha.* ☎ *02/679-1333. Sun–Thurs 9:30am–10pm, Fri 9am–2:30pm, Sat sunset–11pm.*

3 ★★ Ein Yael. The Ein Yael Living Museum is an outdoor facility where visitors learn about ancient art and craft techniques by participating in workshops focusing on

Petting baby goats at the Biblical Zoo.

pottery, weaving, basketry, paper making, wine making, farming, mosaics, baking, and fresco painting. While the kids are busy, parents can explore the remains of a Roman villa dating back to the 2nd century BCE. ⏲ *1½ hr. Manahat, near the Biblical Zoo (see above).* ☎ *02/645-1866. www.einyael.co.il. Admission NIS 35 adults, NIS 40 children. May to Oct, Sat–Thurs 10am–6pm, Fri 10am–4pm; Nov to Apr, Sat–Thurs 10am–4pm, Fri 10am–1pm. It is advisable to call before visiting; inclement weather & private events can cause schedule changes.*

❹ ★★★ Bloomfield Science Museum. This world-class science museum for the whole family just may be in a class of its own, since it focuses on both physical sciences—electricity, water, the brain—and social sciences, such as interpersonal communication and a unique Peace Labyrinth. Special exhibits include the science behind amusement parks, and science and technology in well-known children's stories. Parents may leave older children to engage in interactive activities while they relax in the multimedia Resource Center. All science cards are in Hebrew, English, and Arabic. ⏲ *2 hr. Museum Blvd., Givat Ram.* ☎ *02/654-4888. www.mada. org.il/en. Call ahead for Resource Center hours. Admission NIS 30 adults, NIS 25 children & students, NIS 15 seniors; slightly higher on holidays & during school vacations; free to ASTC passport holders. Mon–Thurs 10am–6pm, Fri 10am–2pm, Sat 10am–4pm; closed Sun.*

❺ ★★ Bible Lands Museum. The museum brings the exhibits to life for children by providing special self-guided tour booklets (in Hebrew and English) that present clues to mysteries that have to be unraveled in the galleries. During school holidays and August, there is also Family Fun: tours led by costumed actors and creative art workshops. There are cafeterias here and at the Israel Museum opposite. ⏲ *2 hr. See p 33, ❷. There is an extra charge for the self-guided mystery tour; call to verify if a particular Family Fun activity is offered in English.*

The Bloomfield Science Museum focuses on both the physical and social sciences.

The whimsical Mifletzet slide.

6 ★★ **The Ruth Youth Wing of the Israel Museum.** One part of the adult museum the kids will probably like is the model of Jerusalem as it likely looked during the Second Temple period. (There is another scale model at City Hall Safra Sq.) But there is also an entire youth wing that is worth checking out, since it is one of the largest of its kind in the world, with daily activities. There is a cafeteria at the Museum. ⏲ *1½ hr. See p 21,* **9** .

7 **Mifletzet slide.** Words cannot do justice to this whimsical, three-tongued slide created by a French artist and nicknamed *mifletzet—* monster. A Jerusalem favorite for more than 20 years. ⏲ *20 min. Rabinowitz Park Kiryat Yovel (just off Herzl Blvd). Free admission.*

What kid doesn't like spaghetti? The restaurant **8** **Spaghettim** is right next door to the Time Elevator and has a menu that will appeal to adults and kids alike. *See p 118. 35 Hillel St.* ☎ *623-5547. $$.*

9 **The Time Elevator.** This 30-minute multimedia presentation of the history of Jerusalem is jazzed up with special chairs and a floor that move in synchronicity with the show. It stars one of Israel's great actors, Chaim Topol (1935–), who played Tevye in *Fiddler on the Roof* on Broadway and film. Parents should exercise discretion with

Children interact with art at the Ruth Youth Wing of the Israel Museum.

younger children or those who suffer from motion sickness. 🕐 *40 min. Beit Agron, 37 Hillel St.* ☎ *02/624-8381, ext. 4. www.time-elevator-jerusalem.co.il/en. Admission NIS 49 adults. Call for schedule.*

⑩ Kad Vachomer. The perfect rainy day activity or a chance for the kids to try their hand at creating their very own "archaeological find." At this paint-your-own ceramics studio, each child (or adult) picks a blank piece of pottery and paints it. An English-speaking art teacher will be glad to offer advice and encouragement. Pieces are left to be glazed and fired and must be picked up several days later. *4 Safra Sq.* ☎ *02/624-5329. Admission NIS 30–NIS 150 adults (depending on size of ceramic painted). Sun, Mon & Wed 2–7pm, Tues & Thurs 11am–11pm; winter Sat 8pm–midnight, closed Fri; summer & school vacations from 11am.*

⑪ ★ Mummy at the Pontifical Biblical Institute Museum. Curious (and brave) little ones will be mesmerized by the Egyptian mummy on display at the museum in the Pontifical Biblical Institute. 🕐 *20 min 3 Emil Botta St.* ☎ *02/625-2843. Mon–Fri 9am–1pm.*

⑫ ★★ The Train Puppet Theater. A former railroad car has found new life as a theater for performances starring puppets and marionettes. Most performances are in Hebrew, but kids

will still enjoy the action. The theater regularly hosts foreign artists, as well as the International Festival of Puppet Theaters. *Liberty Bell Park.* ☎ *02/561-8514. www.train theater.co.il/english. NIS 40–NIS 80 adults. Call or check the website for performance schedules, as well as occasional free street theater.*

⑬ ★★ Hasmonean water tunnels. If your kids liked Hezekiah's Tunnel (see p 18), or did not get to experience it, you can be sure they'll like this underground water system. Parents will marvel at the way ancient engineers employed primitive methods to accomplish the sophisticated feat of tunneling 10 miles underground from either end and still managing to link up in the middle. 🕐 *2 hr. See p 37,* ⑬.

⑭ Ariel Center for Jerusalem in the First Temple Period. The scale model, with audio-visual presentations, of the city of Jerusalem and the Temple in the days of King Solomon will interest older children. Call the museum in advance to ask about special interactive programs. 🕐 *20 min. Bonei Hahomah St., corner of Plugat Hakotel St.* ☎ *02/628-6288. Admission NIS 18 adults; NIS 14 students, children & seniors. Sun–Thurs 9am–4pm, Fri 9am–1pm.* ●

The Egyptian mummy at the Pontifical Biblical Institute.

3 The Best Neighborhood Walks

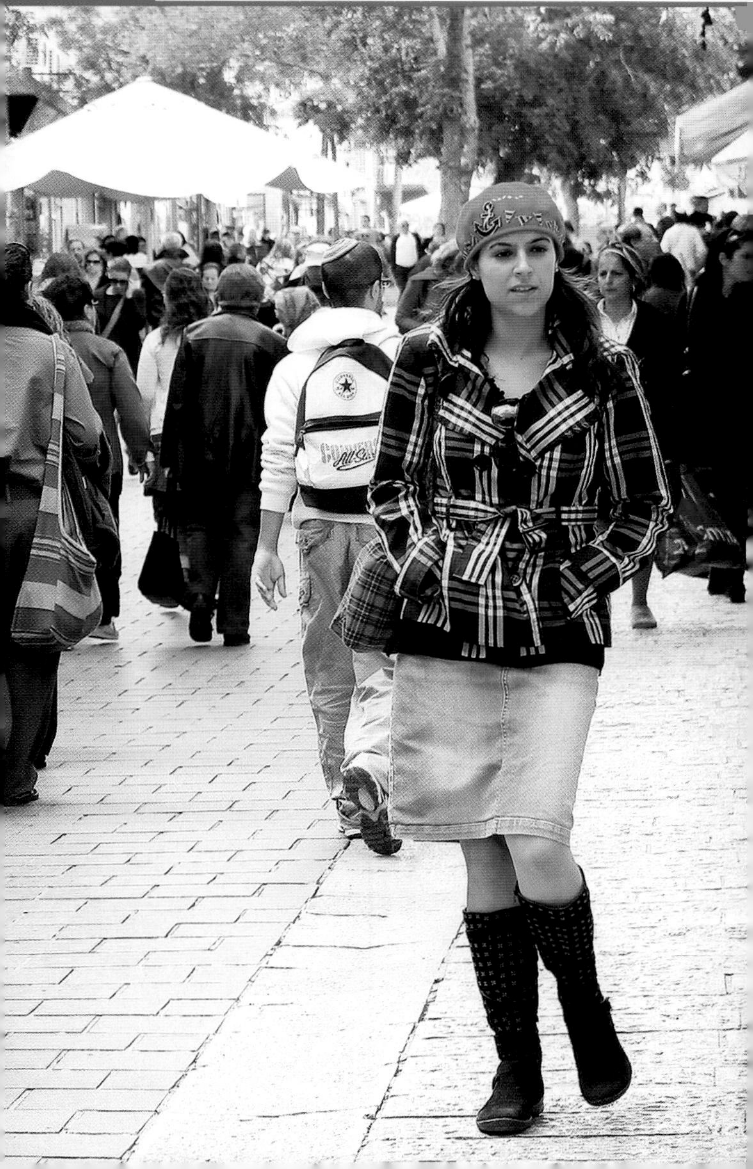

Downtown

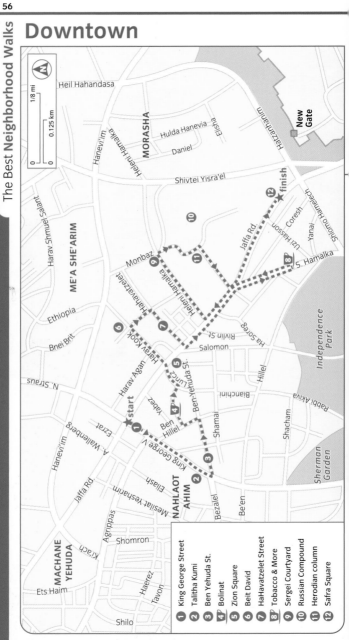

Heil Hahandasa

MORASHA

Hulda Hanevia

Daniel

Shivtei Yisra'el

New Gate

finish

start

1 King George Street
2 Talitha Kumi
3 Ben Yehuda St.
4 Bolinat
5 Zion Square
6 Beit David
7 HaHavatzelet Street
8 Tobacco & More
9 Sergei Courtyard
10 Russian Compound
11 Herodian column
12 Safra Square

Previous page: Ben Yehuda Street in a popular pedestrian mall.

Downtown West Jerusalem was once defined as the triangle formed by King George Street, Ben Yehuda Street, and Jaffa Road. Our walk will take us up King George Street, then down the pedestrian mall to link up with and continue along the eastern extension of Jaffa Road until it ends at City Hall and the boundary between East and West Jerusalem. By incorporating interesting side streets and lanes just north of Jaffa Road, this walk joins seamlessly with the HaNevi'im Street walk (see p 72). Branching off south from Jaffa Road is the historic Nahalat Shiva neighborhood, which has been restored as a commercial and restaurant district. START: **Southwest corner of King George St. & Jaffa Rd.**

① **King George Street.** Named for King George V of England (1865–1936), it is the only street in the capital whose name was not Hebraicized, in honor of the ruling monarch at the time of the British government's pro-Jewish homeland Balfour Declaration. The trilingual stone plaque on the corner building commemorates the 1924 dedication ceremony. *2 King George St.*

Proceed uphill on King George St. to the monument on the sidewalk in front of the plaza.

② ★★ **Talitha Kumi.** When this 19th-century Christian girls' orphanage and school was demolished in

1980 as part of urban renewal, the original facade (including clock and inscription), a chimney, and part of a window were retained from the original Conrad Schick (1822–1901) building and placed as a memorial of sorts at the corner of King George and Ben Yehuda streets. *16 King George St.*

Cross King George St.

③ ★★★ **Ben Yehuda Street.** When this regular street was transformed into a pedestrian mall in 1983, downtown Jerusalem was changed forever. The legendary Café Atara has sadly been replaced by a Burger King, but the rest of the developments have been positive. Strolling down

The façade of Talitha Kumi.

the mall is a city pastime: In good weather, musicians abound and visiting chorale or instrumental groups give impromptu concerts. On late Friday afternoons, a dance party outside Bolinat (see below, ④') ushers in the weekend.

Anytime of day or night, stop in at ④' ★ **Bolinat** for a snack, coffee, or one of the specialty alcoholic shakes; it's open 24 hours. *6 Dorot Rishonim St.* ☎ *02/624-9733. $$.*

⑤ ★ **Zion Square.** This plaza is the Jerusalem equivalent of Tel Aviv's Rabin Square: historically, the venue of choice for political demonstrations for or against government policies. The impressive Sansur Building (2 Ben Yehuda St.), built by a wealthy Bethlehemite who gave it his name, has been a mute witness to many a rally—and unfortunately, some horrific acts of terror. *At the intersection of Ben Yehuda St. & Jaffa Rd.*

Cross Jaffa Rd., walk west a few yards, and turn right on HaRav Kook St. At #9, turn into the lane bearing the name Ticho St.

⑥ ★★ **Beit David.** Just a few steps in, on your right, is the entrance to Beit David, only the fourth neighborhood to be built outside the Old City (at the time, the

late 1870s, a single large courtyard surrounded by apartments was considered a neighborhood). This one is amazingly well preserved—and still occupied—primarily because of its most illustrious previous resident: the first Chief Ashkenazic Rabbi of pre-state Israel, Abraham Isaac Kook (1865–1935). His former office is now a small museum. The pictures in stone next to the second, crenellated entryway tell some of his story. *Free admission. Courtyard always open. Museum Sun–Thurs 9am–4pm, Fri 9am–noon; closed Sat.*

Return to Jaffa Rd. and turn left.

⑦ **HaHavatzelet Street.** This street has also been transformed into a pedestrian mall, as have two of its parallel streets (at least partially). The buildings at 40 and 38 Jaffa Rd. are particularly handsome ones, on a street where it's worth looking up, as well as around.

It might look like simply a small store selling liquor and cigars, but ⑧' ★ **Tobacco & More** is also a nice little cafe with an espresso bar and tables upstairs. Order cheese or chocolate to eat here or take home, and check out the unique wine filling station. *15 Shlomzion Hamalka St.* ☎ *02/625-2886. $$.*

The Renaissance-style Imperial tower at Sergei Courtyard.

Jerusalem Municipality Free Walking Tours

The city of Jerusalem sponsors free walking tours in English most Saturdays at 10am. Tours last between 2 and 3 hours, and depart from Safra Square (24–26 Jaffa Rd.); however, since the routes differ from week to week, it is always best to check the details under the Tourism tab at www.jerusalem.muni.il. The tourist information phone number provided by the website (☎ 02/531-4600) is answered only in Hebrew.

Turn left up Heleni Hamalka St. to #13, on the left.

9 ★★★ **Sergei Courtyard.** This compound, with its Renaissance-style Imperial tower, is like a fairy-tale castle come to life. It was built as part of a sprawling complex of hostels to accommodate thousands of Russian pilgrims (until World War I, Russians composed the largest block of pilgrims to the Holy Land). The buildings surrounding this particular pastoral courtyard were constructed to house Russian royalty. Note especially the twin mini-towers that look like chess rooks: They were outhouses—and one of them is still in use as a public lavatory! The complex is now the headquarters of the Society for the Protection of Nature in Israel; the antique agricultural implements on display in the yard were donated by the legendary General Moshe Dayan (1915–1981). ⏱ *15 min. 13 Heleni Hamalka St.* ☎ *02/625-2357.*

Turn left after exiting the courtyard. Before making an immediate right, at the corner on either side of Heleni Hamalka St., you can see the engraved coats of arms of the Russian Orthodox Church.

10 ★★ **Russian Compound.** The 19th-century series of structures surrounding the Russian Orthodox Holy Trinity Cathedral (see p 42) served the large community of Russian pilgrims in the Holy Land; separate hostels were built for men and women. More than a thousand at a time could stay in the massive building at the southern edge of the compound, which is now at the corner of Heshin Street and Jaffa Road. *1 Heshin St.*

11 ★★ **Herodian column.** Opposite the entrance to the cathedral, just to the left of the entrance to Jerusalem's jail, a low iron fence surrounds a monumental Herodian-era column abandoned in the process of being carved directly from bedrock; it apparently cracked and was simply left in its place. The gate is always unlocked, so you can walk down the steps and get up close.

Walk due east, passing the entrance to the cathedral on the left.

12 ★★ **Safra Square.** The relatively new city hall complex has done an excellent job of incorporating the old into its design. Wander around and find the Archimedes Screw Fountain in Gan Daniel, Jerusalem's oldest public garden (it was far larger when first laid out in 1892; the park is named for Daniel Auster [1893–1962], the city's first Jewish mayor after the establishment of the state). The extreme southwest corner of the square boasts a replica of the famous clover map depicting Jerusalem as the center of the Earth. *Opposite 19 Jaffa Rd.*

Ein Karem

1. Mary's Spring
2. Eden-Tamir Music Center
3. The Church of the Visitation
4. Gorny Convent Grounds
5. Karma
6. The Church of Saint John
7. The Sisters of Sion
8. Observation point
9. Agua

The reputed birthplace of John the Baptist is a picturesque village nestled in a valley between Mt. Herzl on one side and the ridge boasting the renowned Hadassah Medical Center (and Chagall windows) on the other. Now incorporated into Jerusalem, this bucolic suburb of renovated old Arab-style cottages and villas has become one of the city's most desirable residential neighborhoods. On Saturdays, Ein Karem (it means Spring of the Vineyard) fills up with Israelis, while on Sundays, most of the churches and convents that dot the village are closed. START: **Mary's Spring (where Ma'ayan St. dead-ends at Ma'aleh Ha-akhsaniya St.).**

1 ★★ **Mary's Spring.** For such a compact place, Ein Karem affords a multiplicity of terrific, ever-changing views. Our walk starts in the center of town, on Ma'ayan Street, named after the spring where Mary drew water when she came to visit her cousin Elizabeth. According to Christian lore, when Mary was pregnant with Jesus, she came to visit Elizabeth, who was pregnant with John the Baptist: When the two expectant women touched each other's stomachs, the two infants jumped for joy inside their mothers' wombs. It is a highlight of a pilgrimage to drink from the same water source, channeled via an ancient tunnel. 🕐 *10 min. Corner of Ma'ayan & Ma'aleh Ha-akhsaniya sts.*

The site of Mary's Spring.

❷ Eden-Tamir Music Center.
Just opposite the mosque built right over the spring (in Muslim recognition of the sanctity of the site) is a former villa now reconstituted as the Targ Music Center, one of Jerusalem's most delightful venues for recitals and chamber music concerts. *29 HaMa'ayan St. See p 125.*

Walk up the hill from the spring, to the top of the road that passes to the right of the Music Center. You can ascend either via steps or a ramp. Make frequent stops not only to rest, but also to take in the gorgeous views of the houses and church spires below, as well as centuries-old agricultural terraces. *Note: The climb can be very steep for seniors or people out of shape.*

❸ ★★ The Church of the Visitation. This church, commemorating that same visit between the mothers-to-be, belongs—like the

Church of Saint John (see p 62, ❻) to the Franciscan order. The facade is graced by a mosaic depicting Mary of Nazareth visiting her older cousin in Ein Karem, accompanied by three haloed angels. Above the gate is the symbol of the Franciscans, flanked by statues of Elizabeth and Zachariah, John the Baptist's parents. Just inside are more statues of the two pregnant women. The courtyard is adorned with ceramic tiles of the Magnificat, Mary's hymn of thanksgiving, rendered in many languages. There is another mosaic in the church's crypt, as well as lunettes of scenes of the life of John and his parents. The marble altar rests on a carved pedestal with a relief of the Lamb of God, the name John gave Jesus. *At the top of the pedestrian extension of HaMa'ayan St. Daily 8–11:30am & 2:30–5pm.*

❹ Gorny Convent Grounds.
Just above the Church of the Visitation is the sprawling compound known in vernacular Arabic parlance as *Moscow-biya,* since it is the

Mary's Hymn of Thanksgiving at the Church of the Visitation.

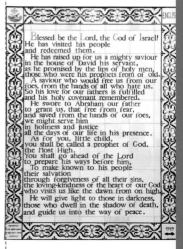

The Church of St. John was built on the spot believed to be where John the Baptist was born.

grounds of the Russian "Gorny" Convent, dominated by the beautiful Russian Orthodox church with golden onion-shaped domes. The resemblance to the Church of Mary Magdalene on the Mount of Olives is not coincidental: The Ein Karem convent was a favorite retreat of Elizabeth, the last czar's sister-in-law; after her husband was assassinated, she actually became a nun and joined the convent, starting to build the large church in memory of her slain husband modeled after the church just outside Jerusalem's walls. Eventually, Elizabeth was buried at the Church of Mary Magdalene, whose dedication she had attended in the previous century. *The enclave of nun's houses, Church of Elizabeth & Zacharias Church are closed to the public. View them from a number of perspectives, including* 🍵, *below.*

Walk back past Mary's Spring to the town center.

🍵 ★ **Karma**, near the intersection of Ma'ayan Street and Ein Karem Road in the center of town, is a good place for a break and some people watching. Service is spotty and the food not cheap, but the *taboon* (stone oven) specialties are quite good and the view

exceptional. *74 Ein Karem Rd.* ☎ *02/643-6643. $$$.*

The Mevo Hasha'ar alleyway (lined with shops and souvenir stalls) leads straight to the gate of the church with the most prominent steeple in the village.

6 **The Church of Saint John.** This magnificent church was built on the spot believed to be where John the Baptist was born. Once again, we encounter ceramic plaques with a prayer in many languages: this time, the Benedictus, in the style of a psalm, proclaimed by John's father when his son was born. The grotto beneath the church contains the remains of a Byzantine mosaic; Roman statuary was also found here and is now on display in the Rockefeller Museum. *Mevo Hasha'ar. Daily 6am–noon & 2–5pm.*

Upon leaving the church courtyard, turn right; this alley leads to a main street (Ein Karem Road), where you turn left and make an immediate right into a short lane. When the lane dead ends, bear right and then left along Derekh Ha'ahayot St., which takes you past open fields along the right—the grounds of the Sisters of Sion Convent.

Walk along the lane on your right; at the end is a great view of the Judean Hills west of Jerusalem.

7 The Sisters of Sion. The entrance to the convent is through a locked gate where Derekh Ha'ahayot Street turns into HaOren Street. The tranquility of the garden is equal to that of the interior of the austere chapel, whose altar is dappled by colored light refracted through twin stained glass windows. Patrons of the convent's guest house enjoy this atmosphere throughout their stay (see p 140). ⏱ ½ *hr. HaOren St. Admission NIS 2 adults. Mon–Thurs 9am–noon & 2–5pm, Sat 9am–5pm; closed Sun. Ring for admission.*

Turn right upon leaving the convent grounds.

8 Observation point. The best view of the town's Russian Orthodox churches can be enjoyed from the vacant lot on HaOren Street opposite Shibboleth Lane. In January, the hills are covered with the delicate white blooms of almond trees.

Pass a 19th-century Greek Orthodox church (closed to the public except on holidays) on the left to complete our loop and end up back in the center of town.

If you finish your walk towards evening and feel like a drink in an intimate atmosphere, **9 Agua** has a pleasant bar on the second floor. *1 Ma'ayan St. ☎ 02/644-9494. $$.*

The Artist Village

A good number of artists—potters, calligraphers, and sculptors—have established studios in their Ein Karem residences; the town organizes frequent festivals showcasing the local crafts. American-born painter Yitzhak Greenfield, whose studio is at 5 HaOren St. (☎ 02/641-6097), and Australian-born culinary creator Hila Solomon, who has a restaurant-by-appointment named Spoons (21 HaOren St.; ☎ 02/623-5778), have particularly lovely refurbished homes and gardens.

A studio in the Artist's Village.

Yemin Moshe–German Colony

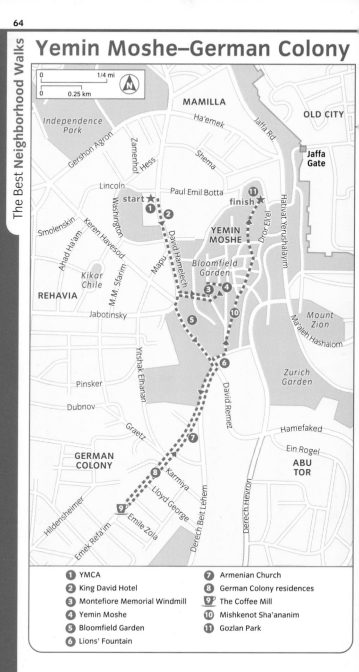

0   1/4 mi
0   0.25 km

MAMILLA

OLD CITY

Independence Park

Ha'emek

Jaffa Rd.

Jaffa Gate

Gershon Agron

Zamenhof   Hess

Shema

Lincoln

Paul Emil Botta

start ★ ①
②

Washington

Mapu

David Hamelech

YEMIN MOSHE

finish ★ ⑪

Dror Eliel

Hativat Yerushalayim

Smolenskin

Keren Hayesod

Ahad Ha'am

M.M. Starim

Bloomfield Garden

Kikar Chile

③ ④

REHAVIA

Jabotinsky

⑤

⑩

Mount Zion

Ma'aleh Hashalom

Yitshak Elhanan

Pinsker

⑥

Zurich Garden

Dubnov

Graetz

⑦

David Remez

Hamefaked

Ein Rogel

ABU TOR

GERMAN COLONY

⑧ Karmiya

Lloyd George

Derech Bett Lehem

Derech Hevron

⑨ The Coffee Mill

Hildensheimer

Emile Zola

Emek Refa'im

① YMCA
② King David Hotel
③ Montefiore Memorial Windmill
④ Yemin Moshe
⑤ Bloomfield Garden
⑥ Lions' Fountain

⑦ Armenian Church
⑧ German Colony residences
⑨ The Coffee Mill
⑩ Mishkenot Sha'ananim
⑪ Gozlan Park

This walk is designed for an afternoon, as it takes us along a garden route with a terrific view of the Old City. But first we visit two very different neighborhoods, with similar beginnings: Both were founded in the 19th century, when jackals roamed the barren countryside that is now home to some of Jerusalem's wealthiest residents. START: **YMCA at the corner of King David & Lincoln Sts.**

1 ★★ YMCA. Surprisingly, one of the most interesting buildings in West Jerusalem is the YMCA—designed by the architects of the Empire State Building and the epitome of modernity when it was built in the 1920s. There is plenty of symbolism meant to reflect inter-religious brotherhood: for example, the 12 windows in the auditorium representing the number of Israelite tribes, Jesus' disciples, and Muhammad's followers. On the floor of the entrance is a copy of the ancient mosaic Madeba Map; another one is in the Cardo in the Jewish Quarter. One could spend hours wandering around the building and its porticos, and marveling at the detail; the view from the tower is also impressive. The elevator is for hotel guest use only. ⏱ *30 min. 26 King David St.* ☎ *02/569-2692. www.ymca3arch. co.il. Admission to tower NIS 5 adults. Hotel open 24 hr.; tower open daily until 8pm.*

Walk across the street to the King David Hotel.

2 ★ King David Hotel. For generations, this has been the hotel of notable and official state visitors to Jerusalem (the King David now shares this distinction with the David Citadel down the street). The lobby has a "walk of fame" with the names and signatures of presidents and celebrities who have been guests. Check out the cozy bar and the terrace with the amazing view; you might want to return for a drink. ⏱ *15 min. 23 King David St.* ☎ *02/ 620-8888. www.danhotels.com.*

Walk down King David St. to the traffic light. Turn left onto Bloomfield St., and you will practically walk into the windmill.

3 Montefiore Memorial Windmill. This windmill was built in 1857 by Sir Moses Montefiore (1784–1885), a British philanthropist who spent 60 of his 101 years building new Jewish communities outside the walls of the Old City, which was overcrowded and becoming unsanitary. The windmill is now a museum

The residences of Yemin Moshe.

The Lions' Fountain, a gift from the German government.

honoring his good works. Some of the money he spent here was bequeathed to him for this purpose by the American Jewish philanthropist Judah Touro (1775–1854).

The plaza in front of the windmill affords magnificent views of the Old City walls and the Hinnom Valley. Walk into the parking lot just north of the windmill and take any of the steps leading down into the Yemin Moshe neighborhood.

④ **Yemin Moshe.** Until 1967, this neighborhood was in the line of fire of Jordanian snipers shooting from the Old City. Only old people who could not afford to move elsewhere lived in the decaying buildings. After the Six Day War, artists and people of means were given permission to occupy the mostly abandoned residences, on the condition that they fixed them up. Now, it is an extremely upscale neighborhood; walk through the pedestrian alleys, admire the reconstruction and gardens, and look for open galleries.

Return to King David St. and turn left.

⑤ **Bloomfield Garden.** Colorful flower beds on your left make your walk down the gentle slope very pleasant. *See p 103,* ⑩.

⑥ **Lions' Fountain.** A gift from the Federal Republic of Germany in 1989, the fountain's water spouts from the mouths of lions, the symbol of Judea/Jerusalem. *Corner of King David and David Remez Sts.*

Continue through the David Remez Square intersection on the side of the gas station; the name of the street will change to Emek Refaim St. At the fork in the road with Derekh Bet Lehem (Bethlehem Road) branching off to the left, you will see a charming stone building on the east side of the street.

⑦ ★ **Armenian Church.** The building with the small belfry is the community meeting house for the Society of the Temple, a German Protestant sect that settled this area in 1873. After the Templers (no connection with the Order of the Knights Templar of the Crusader era) were expelled by the British during the Second World War, the newly formed state of Israel in 1948 gave the building over to the Armenian community, which converted it into a church. *Junction of Emek Refaim St. & Derekh Bet Lehem.*

Continuing on the west side of Emek Refaim St., you will encounter at #6 the first of the imposing

German-style stone houses that were the Templers' homes.

8 German Colony residences. Note the lintels over the main doorways of the impressive houses: They are all engraved with names or sentences from the scriptures, either in Hebrew or German, together with the dates of their construction.

Further southward along Emek Refaim St., the residences change into storefronts.

9 The Coffee Mill is one of Jerusalem's most charming cafes. Choose from the illustrated menu that diagrams exactly what your cup of coffee, hot chocolate, or mocha (hot or cold) will look like. *25 Emek Refaim St.* 📞 *02/566-1665.* $.

If you head back towards King David St. on the east side of Emek Refaim St., you might want to turn right down some of the lanes (Cremieux, Lloyd George) with beautiful homes and gardens. Just before you reach the Armenian Church, you will see large abandoned buildings that served as boarding schools for the Templers. Return to Lions'

The belfry of the Armenian Church.

Saul Bellow and Isaac Stern are a couple of the famous guests who've stayed at Mishkenot Sha'ananim.

Fountain and take the pedestrian path off to the right, which will lead to a parking lot.

10 ★ Mishkenot Sha'ananim. At the north end of the parking lot is a long building with a crenellated roof (reminiscent of the Old City ramparts), which housed the original apartments built more than 150 years ago by Moses Montefiore. Former Jerusalem Mayor Teddy Kollek (1911–2007) had the edifice lovingly restored and turned it into an official municipal guest residence for visiting artists, writers, and musicians; among the luminaries who stayed here were Saul Bellow (1915–2005) and Isaac Stern (1920–2001).

From here, one may return to King David St. or continue through the foot of the Yemin Moshe neighborhood to another verdant park.

11 Gozlan Park. An intimate little gem of a garden tucked away between the King David Hotel and the Old City Walls. *See p 104,* **11**.

Nahla'ot

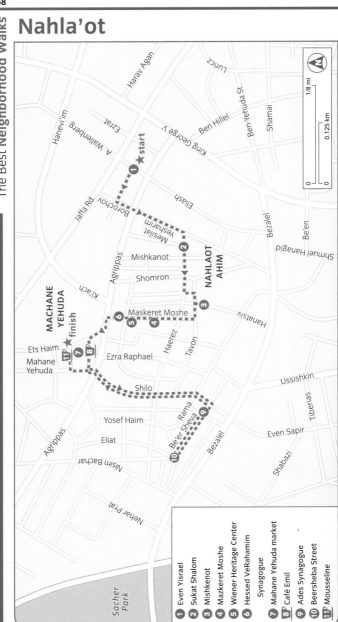

MACHANE
YEHUDA

NAHLAOT
AHIM

Sacher
Park

1. Even Yisrael
2. Sukat Shalom
3. Mishkenot
4. Mazkeret Moshe
5. Wiener Heritage Center
6. Hessed VeRahamim
   Synagogue
7. Mahane Yehuda market
8. Café Emil
9. Ades Synagogue
10. Beersheba Street
11. Mousseline

Τhis walk will take us into the courtyards of the earliest Jewish neighborhoods established outside the Old City walls, in the latter half of the 19th century. A process of gentrification started here about 15 years ago and continues today, resulting in a transformation quite pleasing to the eye. START: **Haim Elboher St. (at Agrippas St.).**

1 Even Yisrael. The lane to the right just west of 8 Agrippas St. leads to a square off to the left that contains a small amphitheater. Pay attention to the photographs mounted on the walls: They are part of the Photos in Stone project that documents the lives of the early pioneers from more than a century ago who left the cramped but protected confines of the Jewish Quarter in the Old City to settle what was then a relative wilderness. These photos will accompany us on our walk. One in particular in the Even Yisrael collection is special: a rare photo capturing David Ben-Gurion (1886–1973), the George Washington of Israel, as a young man—barely recognizable in comparison with the familiar visage of an old man with an unruly white mane.

Walk along the unnamed lane that leads to the square, which takes you to Baruchoff St. (the street sign is not visible), turn left, cross over Agrippas St.,

continue straight (the name of the street will change to Mesilat Yesharim Street), and make the first right, onto Rabbi Aryeh St.

2 Sukat Shalom. This is a typical neighborhood that has retained its character from years gone by: narrow alleys populated by attached whitewashed homes. Note the square on the right with the communal clotheslines propped up 4.6m (12 ft.) high by notched poles.

Continue walking on Rabbi Aryeh St. in the direction we came, then take a left on Shomron St. and an immediate right on Tavor St.

3 Mishkenot. Note the fortress-like walls on the left, punctuated by two imposing arched gates. The first one (1 Tavor St.) is locked, but you can enter the large courtyard from around the corner (Hanetziv St.); the next entryway (no street number) is exactly opposite where Mazkeret Moshe Street dead-ends into Tavor Street. Note the sealed-up

Photographs from Even Yisrael.

cisterns—wells that look like tree stumps, which were once the water source for many neighborhoods like this. There would also have been one communal oven, usually in the basement of the synagogue. These courtyards are inhabited by ultra-Orthodox residents; visitors should dress appropriately. *Tavor St., between Shomron & Mazkeret Moshe sts.*

Exit the huge gateway back onto Tavor St., continue straight along Mazkeret Moshe St. approximately 18m (60 ft.), turn right (up a few stairs) onto Rabbi Aryeh St., and take the first left onto Einayim Lamishpat St.

4 Mazkeret Moshe. This square, now occupied by a kindergarten, was the heart of Mazkeret Moshe—yet another neighborhood (like Yemin Moshe and numerous others) named after the ubiquitous benefactor Moses (Moshe) Montefiore. The legendary philanthropist's photos and biography are posted on the central bulletin board. *16 Einayim Lamishpat St.*

5 Wiener Heritage Center. The beautifully restored building at the northern end of the square is now a center dedicated to preserving the heritage of Jerusalem's older neighborhoods; it is also the headquarters of the Photos in Stone project. *Mazkeret Moshe Square. ☎ 02/622-3267. Hebrew-language slide show NIS 15 adults; by appointment only. The building (including restrooms) is closed to visitors.*

6 ★ Hessed VeRahamim Synagogue. Just behind the Wiener Center is a gem of a synagogue with a facade gilded in silver, a stained glass window, and an array of clock faces with the hands set to prayer times. One of the first synagogues outside the Old City, the "Kindness and Mercy" Synagogue is still used by members of the Sephardic community. *Carmel St. (between #12 & #20).*

Turn right onto Mazkeret Moshe St. from Carmel St., and you will find yourself at the southern (Agrippas St.) entrance to the outdoor Mahane Yehuda market.

7 Mahane Yehuda market. See p 28, **7**.

Take a break at **8 ★ Café Emil,** a popular eatery run by an Israeli who lived for quite a few years in the U.S. The house specialty is the green shakshuka (herbed omelet). Right across the street you can't

The entrance to Hessed VeRahamim Synagogue.

Natural juices from Azrieli, Jerusalem's famed citron medicine man.

miss the array of refreshing natural juices hawked by Azrieli, Jerusalem's famed citron medicine man. Watch as people consult Azrieli, who will "prescribe" one of his drinks to cure the reported malady (one concoction treats 119 diseases, he claims). You can get a free taste of any of the beverages, or buy a very small cup for only NIS 2. *8 HaEgoz St.* ☎ *077/700-3047. $$.*

Exit the market via Mahane Yehuda St., cross over Agrippas St., and continue down Shiloh St. to the corner of Beersheba St.

9 ★ Ades Synagogue. This landmark synagogue was established in 1901 by immigrants from Aleppo, Syria, who brought with them a 10th-century Bible, the oldest one known to be in existence. (The original was donated to the Israel Museum; the congregation retained a copy.) If it is locked, take a peek through an open window: The interior is richly decorated. *Corner of Shiloh & Beersheba sts.*

10 Beersheba Street. Take a stroll down one of the most pleasant, recently gentrified boulevards in Nahla'ot. If you take a left when Beersheba Street dead-ends, you will hit a major thoroughfare, Bezalel Street. If you turn right on Bezalel Street and go downhill, you will be rewarded with some nice views ahead of you of the Supreme Court (see p 45) and the Knesset (see p 45).

Backtrack to Shiloh St. and turn left until it dead ends at Agrippas St. Turn left and left again onto the market's Mahane Yehuda St.

Cool off at **11 Mousseline,** where you'll find great French ice-cream cones in flavors you may have never tasted—basil and cardamom are two of the most unusual, and best. *17 Ha'egoz St.* ☎ *02/500-3601. $.*

Season of Penitence Tours

In the month preceding the Day of Atonement (Yom Kippur), people strolling through this neighborhood (and the Old City) after dark may notice groups on walking tours at unusual hours. Traditionally, Jewish penitential prayers are recited at daybreak during the month of Elul (corresponding to Aug–Sept); synagogue groups from around the country journey to the Holy City at night and stay for prayers at the Western Wall as the sun rises.

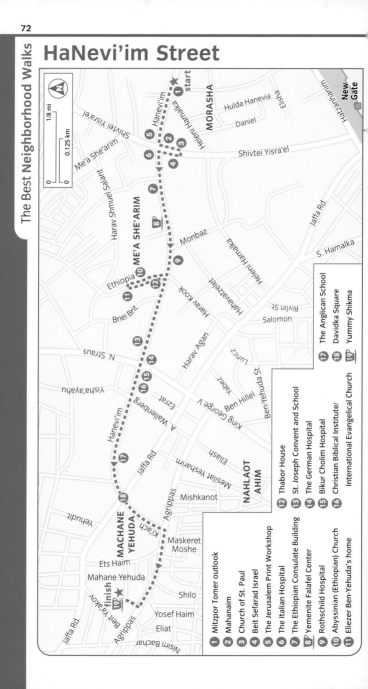

HaNevi'im Street

1 Mitzpor Tomer outlook
2 Mahanaim
3 Church of St. Paul
4 Beit Sefarad Israel
5 The Jerusalem Print Workshop
6 The Italian Hospital
7 The Ethiopian Consulate Building
8 Yemenite Falafel Center
9 Rothschild Hospital
10 Abyssinian (Ethiopian) Church
11 Eliezer Ben-Yehuda's home
12 Thabor House
13 St. Joseph Convent and School
14 The German Hospital
15 Bikur Cholim Hospital
16 Christian Biblical Institute/
International Evangelical Church
17 The Anglican School
18 Davidka Square
19 Yummy Shikma

This historic street, which wends it way from the border of the Old and New cities to the heart of West Jerusalem, contains some of the most beautiful buildings built in Israel around the turn of the 20th century. The "Street of the Prophets" runs parallel to Jaffa Road until the two meet at Davidka Square. START: **Mitzpor Tomer, at the corner of HaNevi'im St. & Rte. 1.**

❶ ★★ Mitzpor Tomer outlook. Although the platform is only slightly above street level, there is still a magnificent view to the east and south, encompassing the Dome of the Rock, the Old City walls, and the exquisite upper exterior of Notre Dame.

Walk straight westward along HaNevi'im St. to the corner of Shivtei Yisrael St. Turn left and look at the building opposite #25.

❷ ★★ Mahanaim. This was the elegant residence of some of the most prominent people in the modern history of Israel. The wealthy German Christian banker who built it named it for the biblical (book of Genesis) place Jacob called "God's camps." *Note:* Casual visitors may view the lintel and exterior from just inside the outer gate but are generally not permitted to pass through security to enter the grounds. *36 Shivtei Yisrael St.*

❸ ★★ Church of St. Paul. This Anglican church—one of the first houses of worship built outside the Old City—is a real gem. When it was established, in the late 19th century, it was just a short walk across barren land from Damascus Gate. It is now a house of worship shared by Christian groups ranging from Finnish evangelists to Reformed Baptists. *32 Shivtei Yisrael St.* ☎ *054/428-2803.*

Look over to the east side of the street.

❹ ★ Beit Sefarad Israel. This lovely building with a Star of David on its facade currently serves as a center for creating cultural and spiritual bridges between the Spanish people and the Jewish state. *23 Shivtei Yisrael St.* ☎ *077/344-3370.*

Return to HaNevi'im St. and cross to the north side of the street.

❺ The Jerusalem Print Workshop. This lovely 19th-century Ottoman home is now an art center dedicated to the advancement of printmaking. The gallery displays

The 19th-century Church of St. Paul.

The Italian Hospital is an architectural landmark designed by Barluzzi.

temporary exhibits from Israel's largest archival collection of original prints. ⏱ *20 min. 38 Shivtei Yisrael St., corner of HaNevi'im St.* ☎ *02/ 628-8614. Free admission. Gallery Sun–Thurs 8am–3pm.*

Cross Shivtei Yisrael St.

⑥ ★★★ The Italian Hospital. Now part of Israel's Ministry of Education headquarters, this large former hospital by Barluzzi (1884–1960, see Three Architects Who Transformed Jerusalem, p 48) ranks among the most magnificent buildings in the city. Although only a few of the old coat-of-arms tiles remain (look high up along the walls), the building's towers and chapel still have the ability to transport passersby hundreds of years back in time. The modern curved building on the opposite side of the plaza was designed to complement and frame the architectural masterpiece. The colorful mosaic in the corner is contemporary. *Northwest corner of Shivtei Yisrael & HaNevi'im sts.*

⑦ ★ The Ethiopian Consulate Building. There has been a special relationship between Israel and Ethiopia since the legendary days of King Solomon and the Queen of Sheba. Tradition says Ethiopia's monarchs down to the 20th century are descended from the son of their union; their royal symbol is the Lion of Judah, portrayed in the mosaic that adorns the center of this large edifice, which served as the Ethiopian consulate in the early 20th century. Sadly, the interior of the building has deteriorated into slummy apartments. *38–40 HaNevi'im St.*

Seize this opportunity to taste some of the best falafel in Jerusalem, at the ☕ **Yemenite Falafel Center** (sign in Hebrew only). There may be a line, but it moves quickly—and the owner will give you a falafel ball or two to snack on while you wait. You can order full or half portions of falafel stuffed into pita, or wrapped in a *lafa* (like a large, soft flour taco). *42 HaNevi'im St. No phone. $.*

Cross over to the south side of the street.

⑨ Rothschild Hospital. Stop for a moment at the first Jewish hospital built outside the Old City, funded by the philanthropist Baron Jacob de Rothschild and dedicated in 1888 (it had been operating in the Old City since 1835); note his name inscribed in the stone next to the gate. *37 HaNevi'im St.*

Re-cross the street and turn right at Ethiopia St. Mind the traffic: It is a narrow street with no sidewalks.

⑩ ★★★ Abyssinian (Ethiopian) Church. Enter the gate under the Ethiopian Lion of Judah to visit this unique church: Built in the round, the altar—termed the "holy of holies" and modeled on the incense altar of the Temple during the time of Jesus—is in the center, under the dome. Note the throne-like chair opposite the altar; leaning against the wall on both its sides are the long canes used ritually by worshipers during services. ⏱ *20 min. 10 Ethiopia St. Daily until the evening.*

Cross to the west side of the street.

⑪ Eliezer Ben-Yehuda's home. Ben-Yehuda (1858–1922), the father of the modern spoken Hebrew language and the man after whom Jerusalem's main pedestrian

The dome of the Abyssinian Church.

mall is named, lived here. He is depicted on the Picture of Stone. *11 Ethiopia St. No entry.*

Walk back to HaNevi'im St. Peek in at the side of the house on the northwest corner, then turn right to view the front.

⑫ ★★ Thabor House. Now the Swedish Theological Institute, this building was the home of the renowned architect Conrad Schick (see Three Architects Who Transformed Jerusalem, p 48). The name and one of the biblical references thereto, Psalms 89:13, are inscribed on the lintel over the main door. See how many theological symbols—like the seashell and Alpha-Omega—you can spot on the walls of this fascinating residence. *58 HaNevi'im St.*

⑬ St. Joseph Convent and School. Unfortunately, this splendid French Renaissance–style building is mostly blocked from view by a wall and solid gate. The courtyard next door is interesting: The home at the end of the garden belonged to the British artist William Holman Hunt (1827–1910), while the bungalow was the residence of "Rahel" (1890–1931), one of Israel's foremost poets. *64–66 HaNevi'im St.*

Cross the street and walk to the southeast corner of HaNevi'im and Strauss sts.

⑭ ★ The German Hospital. Now a wing of the Orthodox Jewish hospital across the street, this hospital was previously run by the Old City's Deaconess Sisters nursing order. The building, designed by Conrad Schick (see sidebar, p 48), is in the style of a church. *Southeast corner of HaNevi'im & Strauss sts.*

Cross Strauss St., staying on the south side of HaNevi'im St., then turn left and walk 15m (50 ft.) down the hill.

The entrance to the Bikur Cholim Hospital.

⑮ ★ Bikur Cholim Hospital.
The main building of the hospital, which was founded in the Jewish Quarter of the Old City in 1857, was built in the first quarter of the 20th century. The magnificent doors of beaten bronze portray the symbols of the 12 tribes of Israel and passages from the prophet Isaiah. *5 Strauss St.*

Retrace your steps back to HaNevi'im St. and turn left.

⑯ ★ Christian Biblical Institute/International Evangelical Church. Adjacent to the hospital is an evangelical center and seminary built in the early 20th century by an American missionary organization. The interior of the church boasts a beautiful wooden ceiling. ⏱ *15 min. 55 HaNevi'im St.*

Cross to the north side of the street.

⑰ The Anglican School. The size of this spacious campus, once the grounds of the Anglican Hospital, reflects the former grandeur of the British Empire. The buildings date back to 1896. *82 HaNevi'im St.*

⑱ Davidka Square. This square's name derives from the improvised artillery ordnance the Israelis used to defend the city in the 1948 War of Independence. For decades, an example of this piece of primitive firepower was on display here. At press time, the square was under major renovation. *Intersection of HaNevi'im St. & Jaffa Rd.*

Just across Jaffa Road and up Kiach Street to Agrippas Street lies the embarrassment of riches in the Mahane Yehuda market (p 28, ⑦); if you're here on a Friday afternoon towards sunset, the prices sink to ridiculous lows—and you might catch the Hassidim blowing a tin horn to signal stall owners to pack up for the Sabbath. A terrific ethnic treat may be sampled at **⑲ ★★ Yummy Shikma,** a Georgian bakery that serves up terrific burekas from the region of the Caucuses. Wash down your phyllo dough snack with a bottle of tarragon soda. *5 Hashikma St. (corner of Haeshkol St.).* ☎ *02/537-3630. $. Kosher.* ●

West Jerusalem Shopping

Archie Granot 3
Artists' House Gallery 4
Avi Biran 28
Chocolat 17
Darian Armenian
  Ceramics 16
Educational Bookshop 13
Elia Photo Service 22
Gaia Smith 29
Galeria Me'atzvim 31
Intira 2
Israel Museum 1

Jerusalem Gates Souvenir 33
Jerusalem Pottery 23
Khader M. Baidun
  & Sons 24
Klein 9
LiveO 20
Mazettim 7
Melia Art & Training Center 21
Mira Gallery 25
Nekker Glass Factory 11
Oded Davidson 30
Palestinian Pottery 12

Shoshana 26
Smoke Shop 19
Society for the Protection
  of Nature in Israel 14
Sunbula 27
Tania's Shop 10
Teller 5
Teva Naot 8
The Coffee Mill 32
The Natural Choice 6
Winery 18
Yad Lakashish 15

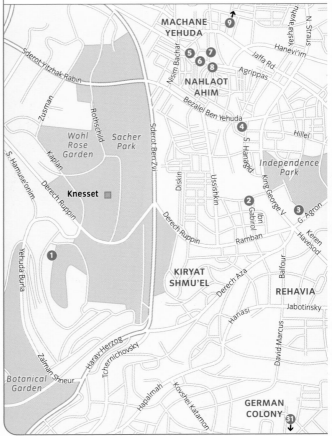

Previous page: Spices for sale at Mahane Yehuda market.

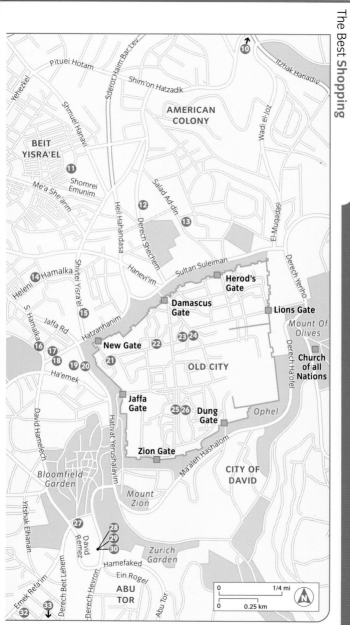

East Jerusalem Shopping

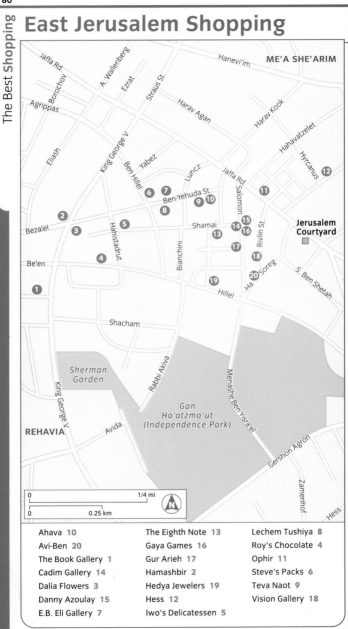

Ahava 10	The Eighth Note 13	Lechem Tushiya 8
Avi-Ben 20	Gaya Games 16	Roy's Chocolate 4
The Book Gallery 1	Gur Arieh 17	Ophir 11
Cadim Gallery 14	Hamashbir 2	Steve's Packs 6
Dalia Flowers 3	Hedya Jewelers 19	Teva Naot 9
Danny Azoulay 15	Hess 12	Vision Gallery 18
E.B. Eli Gallery 7	Iwo's Delicatessen 5	

Shopping Best Bets

Best **Vintage Store**
★ Tania's Shop, *21 Haganah St.*
(p 88)

Best Place for **Artistic Judaica**
★★★ E.B. Eli Gallery, *20 Ben Yehuda St.; 18 King David St. (p 86)*

Best **Armenian Ceramics**
★★★ Palestinian Pottery,
14 Nablus Rd. (p 82)

Best **Cheese Shop**
★★ Mazettim, *13 HaShezif St.*
(p 83)

Best **"Good Deed" Shopping**
★★★ Yad Lakashish (Lifeline for the Old), *14 Shivtei Yisrael St.*
(p 86)

Best **Chocolate Shop**
★★ Roy's Chocolate, *11 Hillel St.*
(p 84)

Best Place for **Packs, Outdoor Gear & Luggage**
★★ Steve's Packs, *11 Ben Hillel St.;
Malha Mall (p 87)*

Best **Olive Oil Products**
★★ LiveO, *Alrov Mamilla Blvd.*
(p 87)

Best **Puzzles**
★★★ Gaya Games, *7 Yoel Salomon St. (p 85)*

Best **Wine Shop**
★★ Avi Ben, *22 Rivlin St.;
3 Ha'armonim St. (p 88)*

Best **Dead Sea Products**
★★ Ahava, *Alrov Mamilla Blvd.*
(p 84)

Best **Browsing**
★★ Book Gallery (books), *6 Schatz St. (p 83);* The Eighth Note (music), *12 Shammai St. (p 87)*

Best **Greeting Card Selection**
★ Gur Arieh, *8 Yoel Salomon St.*
(p 83)

A selection of wines from Avi Ben.

Shopping A to Z

Travel Tip

Only websites in English have been listed. If a Hebrew home page comes up, look for the word English, or an American or British flag. If the Contact Us page consists of a form to fill out rather than an e-mail address, you are better off phoning. And there's no guarantee that you'll get a reply to a direct e-mail in English, either.

Antiquities
★★ Khader M. Baidun & Sons
OLD CITY—One of the best-known antiquities dealers in the Old City, the Baidun family has some museum-quality pieces. *20 Via Dolorosa.* ☎ *02/626-1469. www.baidun.com. AE, MC, V. Map p 78.*

Armenian Ceramics
★ Darian Armenian Ceramics
DOWNTOWN—The only gallery dedicated to this craft in West Jerusalem, Darian has the widest selection of Armenian ceramics with Jewish themes. *12 Shlomzion Hamalka St.* ☎ *02/623-4802. AE, DC, MC, V. Map p 78.*

Antiquities from Khader M. Baidun.

★★ Jerusalem Pottery OLD
CITY—Located near the sixth Station of the Cross in the Old City, this shop is owned by the renowned Karakashian family and features the traditional bird, animal, and floral designs made famous by this Armenian ceramic tile art form. *15 Via Dolorosa.* ☎ *02/626-1587. www. jerusalempottery.biz. AE, MC, V. Map p 78.*

★★★ Palestinian Pottery EAST
JERUSALEM—The art of the Balian family was exhibited in the Smithsonian Museum in Washington and graces the residence of the president of Israel. The store contains a small museum of their classic pieces. You can order personalized items that make great gifts. *14 Nablus Rd. (opposite the U.S. Consulate in East Jerusalem).* ☎ *02/628-2826. www.armenianceramics.com. AE, DC, MC, V. Map p 78.*

Bakeries
★ Lechem Tushiya DOWNTOWN—
Good breads and pastries from a well-regarded national chain. *21 Ben Yehuda St. (pedestrian mall).*

☎ 02/624-5282. Kosher. AE, DC, MC, V. Map p 80.

★ **The Natural Choice** MAHANE YEHUDA—The best place in the city for spelt and other low-gluten baked goods, this bakery supplies quite a few natural food stores. *111 Agrippas St.* ☎ *02/622-3229. www. natural-choice.co.il. Kosher. AE, DC, MC, V. Map p 78.*

★★ **Teller** MAHANE YEHUDA—One of the city's most popular bakeries for French-style breads, it supplies many of the city's best restaurants. Breads and rolls are half-price at 6:45pm. *74 Agrippas St.* ☎ *02/622-3227. Kosher. AE, DC, MC, V. Map p 78.*

Books
★★ **The Book Gallery** DOWN-TOWN—With tens of thousands of used, rare, and antique books in stock, this cavernous store is a bibliophile's paradise. Overstuffed easy chairs and sofas make browsing comfortable. *6 Schatz St. (corner of 26 King George St.).* ☎ *02/623-1087. www.bookgallery.co.il. AE, DC, MC, V. Map p 80.*

★★ **Educational Bookshop** EAST JERUSALEM—Located on the main shopping street of East Jerusalem, this store contains many books on the Middle East you will not find in West Jerusalem—but also many you might, since it admirably carries authors writing about both sides of the conflict. *22 Salaheddin St.* ☎ *02/628-3704. www.educationalbook shop.com. AE, MC, V. Map p 78.*

★ **Gur Arieh** NAHALAT SHIVA—Owner Fredi Engelberg, originally from Brooklyn, stocks maps and guidebooks, as well as old and new books and magazines. She is also a fountain of knowledge about Jerusalem. *8 Yoel Salomon St.* ☎ *02/625-7486. MC, V. Map p 80.*

Customers can sit and browse at The Book Gallery.

Ceramics
★ **Cadim Gallery** NAHALAT SHIVA—This cooperative gallery features the work of Israeli ceramicists whose pieces are exhibited throughout the world. *4 Yoel Salomon St.* ☎ *02/623-4869. AE, DC, MC, V. Map p 80.*

★★ **Gaia Smith** HEBRON ROAD—Ms. Smith's unique creations are developing quite a following; the incredible detail in her work reflects the artist's consummate skill. *House of Quality, 12 Hebron Rd. (opposite the Cinematheque).* ☎ *054/591-0533. www.gaiajudaica.com. No credit cards. Map p 78.*

Cheese
★★ **Mazettim** MAHANE YEHUDA—Owner Itzik left the world of high-tech to become a cheese monger. He also carries a select assortment of boutique Israeli wines and olive oils. *13 HaShezif St., Mahane Yehuda market.* ☎ *02/623-5103. AE, MC, V. Map p 78.*

Chocolate
★★ **Chocolat** DOWNTOWN—The latest entry to burst on the Jerusalem chocolate scene, this cafe/store also boasts a French-trained pastry

chef. Drink the rich chocolate hot on a chilly day. *22 Shlomo Hamelekh St.* ☎ *02/563-5957. Kosher. AE, DC, MC, V. Map p 78.*

★★ **Roy's Chocolate** DOWN-TOWN—Delicious chocolates, truffles, liqueurs, and more; taste some samples and check out the refrigerated section. *11 Hillel St.* ☎ *077/559-4779. Kosher. AE, DC, MC, V. Map p 80.*

Coffee
★★ **The Coffee Mill** GERMAN COLONY—An intimate coffee shop with more varieties of coffee beans per square foot than its competitors, and a menu with handy diagrams explaining the coffees served by the cup. *23 Emek Refaim St.* ☎ *02/566-1665. Kosher. AE, MC, V. Map p 78.*

Dead Sea Products
★★ **Ahava** DOWNTOWN/MAMILLA—Factory outlet stores carrying the best quality health and beauty products manufactured from Dead Sea minerals. *5 Ben Yehuda St. (pedestrian mall).* ☎ *02/624-5282. AE, DC, MC, V. Map p 80; Alrov Mamilla Blvd.* ☎ *02/623-4289. AE, DC, MC, V. Map p 80.*

Delicatessen
★★★ **Hess** DOWNTOWN—Hess's own sausage factory produces a wide variety of deli cold cuts to take home or eat here. Locals come here on Friday to take cooked foods home for the Sabbath. *See p 80.*

★★★ **Iwo's Delicatessen** DOWNTOWN—The city's best purveyor of (mostly) non-kosher meats and gourmet products. *7 Shammai St.* ☎ *02/623-4676. Kosher & non-kosher. AE, DC, MC, V. Map p 80.*

Department Stores
★ **Hamashbir** DOWNTOWN—Jerusalem's first American-style department store, it also carries souvenir-type gifts and has a supermarket in the basement. There is also a branch at the Malha Mall. *20 King George St. (opposite Ben Yehuda pedestrian mall).* ☎ *02/624-0511. AE, DC, MC, V. Map p 80.*

Disposable Goods
★ **Society for the Protection of Nature in Israel** RUSSIAN COMPOUND—In addition to a small selection of maps, the organization's store sells biodegradable picnic-ware (made of recycled sugar cane stalks). *13 Heleni Hamalka St.* ☎ *02/625-7682. No credit cards. Map p 78.*

The Coffee Mill has dozens of different kinds of coffee beans available.

Customer Service & Bargaining

While shopping can be a big treat in Jerusalem, customer service is still pretty much a foreign custom. Don't be surprised if a store clerk in West Jerusalem is too busy on the phone with a personal call to attend to you or to ring up your purchase.

In the Arab *souk* (bazaar), a store owner might invite you to sit down and drink Turkish coffee; it is often difficult not to buy something if you accept the invitation, but it is all part of the experience if the man seems genuinely friendly. Bargaining is de rigueur: It is truly not insulting to offer less than half of the seller's opening price or to walk away if the price does not come down enough. In the Old City, look for items made of mother-of-pearl and olive wood, as well as religious objects.

Fashion

★★ **Galeria Me'atzvim** MALHA MALL—Designers' Gallery showcases a bevy of Israeli couturiers. If you can't find what you want here, there are other excellent shops on the same level in the mall. *Malha Mall.* ☎ *02/679-4082. AE, DC, MC, V. Map p 78.*

Flowers

★★ **Dalia Flowers** DOWNTOWN—A friendly downtown shop that will include other gifts with your bouquet. It also offers international delivery (flowers only). *27 King George St. (corner of Hillel St.).* ☎ *800/220-009 or 02/623-4596. AE, DC, MC, V. Map p 80.*

Games & Toys

★★ **Gaya Games** NAHALAT SHIVA—Beautifully designed and crafted puzzlers, brainteasers, and novelty gift items, perfect for rainy days and waiting in airport terminals. The "Art of Thinking" store (as it calls itself) carries both original games and classics. *7 Yoel Salomon St.* ☎ *02/625-1515. www.gaya-game.com. AE, DC, MC, V. Map p 80.*

Gifts & Souvenirs

★★ **Intira** REHAVIA—This upscale gift store is designed like an art gallery. An entire floor is dedicated to fine cookware; there are also clever gadgets galore. *27 Keren Kayemet St.* ☎ *02/563-7749. AE, DC, MC, V. Map p 78.*

★★ **Jerusalem Gates Souvenir** HEBRON ROAD—Located in a suburb on the way to Bethlehem, this is like a supermarket version of an Old City gifts and souvenir shop, with the addition of some very large and unusual works of art. Bargain as if in the open market. *1 Daniel Yanovski St. (corner of Hebron Rd.).* ☎ *02/672-7290. AE, DC, MC, V. Map p 78.*

★★ **Mira Gallery** JEWISH QUARTER—This very upscale shop carries designer jewelry, art, and Judaica. It has an antiquities license and specializes in ancient coins set into jewelry. *6 Bet El St.* ☎ *02/626-4117. www.mira.co.il. AE, MC, V. Map p 78.*

★ **Shoshana** JEWISH QUARTER—This is the place to come for smaller souvenirs to bring home as gifts. Prices are low, and American-born owner Don Bernstein will be glad to make suggestions, as well as ship

Galeria Me'atzvim is home to a number of Israeli couturiers.

overseas. *16 Tiferet Israel Rd.* ☎ *02/628-1015. www.shoshanagifts.com. AE, DC, MC, V. Map p 78.*

★★★ **Yad Lakashish** DOWNTOWN—The not-for-profit Lifeline for the Old gift shop has handcrafted items for every age, taste, and budget. *14 Shivtei Yisrael St.* ☎ *02/628-7829. AE, DC, MC, V. Map p 78.*

Glass

★★ **Nekker Glass Factory** ME'AH SHE'ARIM—Observe skilled glassblowers creating delicate pieces with the feel of antiquity about them, and purchase items at a fraction of their regular price in retail stores. No sign on the door. *6 Bet Yisrael St.* ☎ *02/582-9683. No credit cards. Map p 78.*

Jewelry

★★ **Hedya Jewelers and the Sarah Einstein Collection** DOWNTOWN—These talented designers create unique pieces reflecting a gamut of Middle East traditions. *23 Hillel St. (in the passageway between Hillel & Shammai sts.).* ☎ *02/622-1151. AE, DC, MC, V. Map p 80.*

★★ **Ophir** DOWNTOWN—A very nice collection of original and

antique pieces; do not miss the annex next to the storefront and through the foyer leading into the building. *38 Jaffa Rd.* ☎ *02/624-9078. www.ophir-jewelry.com. AE, DC, MC, V. Map p 80.*

Judaica

★★ **Danny Azoulay** NAHALAT SHIVA—Azoulay's small shop carries his hand-painted porcelain and fine ceramic Judaica, as well as papercuts and illuminated manuscripts by some of the country's best calligraphers. *5 Yoel Salomon St.* ☎ *02/623-3918. AE, DC, MC, V. Map p 80.*

★★★ **E.B. Eli Gallery** DOWNTOWN—Forget everything you knew about designs for *hannukiyot,* mezuzahs, etc.: The pieces here will blow you away. The gallery also carries antiques and Oriental carpets. *20 Ben Yehuda St.* ☎ *02/625-3103; 18 King David St.* ☎ *02/623-1030. AE, DC, MC, V. Map p 80.*

Museum Shops

★★★ **Artists' House Gallery** DOWNTOWN—This gallery displays the work of hundreds of juried Israeli artists, ranging from the famous to the up-and-coming. A great way to get acquainted with, and acquire, some of Israel's best. *12 Shmuel Hanagid St.* ☎ *02/625-3653. www.art. org.il/en. No credit cards. Map p 78.*

Ophir has original and antique pieces of jewelry.

Archie Granot produces some of Israel's best paper art.

★★★ Israel Museum MUSEUM ROW—A great collection of posters, as well as reproductions of Judaica, antiquities, and works of leading Israelis artists. *Ruppin St.* ☎ *02/670-8811. www.imj-shop.co.il/eng. AE, DC, MC, V. Map p 78.*

Music
★★★ The Eighth Note DOWNTOWN—The best place to shop for music CDs, with state-of-the-art listening stations throughout the store. *12 Shammai St.* ☎ *02/624-8020. AE, DC, MC, V. Map p 80.*

Olive Oil Products
★★ LiveO MAMILLA—In addition to virgin olive oil and olive-based foodstuffs, this store owned by a kibbutz in southern Israel also carries health and beauty products made with olive oil. *Alrov Mamilla Blvd.* ☎ *02/624-6699. www.liveo.co.il. Kosher. AE, DC, MC, V. Map p 78.*

Olive Wood Products
★★ Klein BAR ILAN—Jerusalem's primary factory for olive wood products with Jewish motifs has a showroom that offers good value. (The city's Christian olive wood products are mostly manufactured in Bethlehem.) *3 Ziv Street,* ☎ *02/538-8784. MC, V. Map p 78.*

Packs, Outdoor Gear & Luggage
★★ Steve's Packs DOWNTOWN—A variety of day and overnight packs can be found at the factory outlet store just off the Ben Yehuda pedestrian mall, while a full range of camping gear (including hiking boots) and carry-on luggage is available at the Malha Mall store. *11 Ben Hillel St.* ☎ *02/624-8302; Malha Mall.* ☎ *02/679-3434. AE, DC, MC, V. Map p 80.*

Palestinian Crafts & Embroidery
★★ Melia Art & Training Center OLD CITY—A leading not-for-profit shop carrying traditional embroidery on clothing and other woven goods, including wall hangings. The annex next door sells unusual Palestinian snacks and sweets. *Casa Nova Rd. (Frere's St., inside the Old City's New Gate).* ☎ *02/628-1377. Map p 78.*

★ Sunbula GERMAN COLONY—In addition to embroidery, this not-for-profit shop sells a variety of inexpensive handmade crafts and gift items. *St. Andrew's Scottish Guest House, 1 David Remez St.* ☎ *02/672-1707. AE, MC, V. Map p 78.*

Papercuts
★★★ Archie Granot REHAVIA—Granot is considered the top practitioner in Israel of this art form, and his work is priced accordingly. A

visit to his gallery is like entering a museum. *1 Agron St.* ☎ *02/625-2210. www.archiegranot.com. AE, MC, V. Map p 78.*

Photography

★★★ **Elia Photo Service** OLD CITY—Browse and buy amazing reprints of old photographs of Jerusalem—rare snapshots of history. *14 Al Khanka St., Christian Quarter.* ☎ *02/628-2074. AE, DC, MC, V. Map p 78.*

★★★ **Vision Gallery** NAHALAT SHIVA—Neil Folberg, noted for his landscapes and photographs of the Jewish world, is the owner of this gallery that exhibits his work and that of other contemporary photographers. *18 Yosef Rivlin St.* ☎ *02/622-2253. www.visiongallery.com. AE, DC, MC, V. Map p 80.*

Sandals & Footwear

★★ **Teva Naot** DOWNTOWN—Featuring one of Israel's top brands, this store also carries many of the leading international brands. *7 Ben Yehuda St. (pedestrian mall).* ☎ *02/625-3012. AE, DC, MC, V. Map p 78.*

The silver work from Oded Davidson is of museum quality.

Silversmiths

★★ **Avi Biran** HOUSE OF QUALITY—An award-winning silversmith whose pieces, like those of his colleague and neighbor Oded, are not inexpensive. *12 Hebron Rd.* ☎ *02/679-1082. AE, DC, MC, V. Map p 78.*

★★ **Oded Davidson** HEBROD ROAD—One of Israel's most highly regarded silversmiths, his delicately engraved pieces are prized by

collectors and museums. *12 Hebron Rd.* ☎ *02/673-7626. AE, DC, MC, V. Map p 78.*

Tobacconists

★★ **Smoke Shop** DOWNTOWN/MAMILLA—Cuban cigars are legal in Israel, and this is an ideal place to try before you invest: There are very comfortable leather couches in the rear of the store where you can smoke at your leisure. *Alrov Mamilla Blvd.* ☎ *02/625-5570; 4 Ben Yehuda St.* ☎ *02/625-0501. www.smoke shop.co.il. AE, DC, MC, V. Map p 78.*

Vintage Stores

★★ **Tania's Shop** FRENCH HILL—An honest-to-goodness neighborhood second-hand store, not far from the Regency Hotel. There are some real finds if you browse carefully. *21 Haganah St., second floor of French Hill strip mall.* ☎ *02/581-7397. No credit cards. Map p 78.*

Wine & Liquor

★★ **Avi-Ben** NAHALAT SHIVA—Two conveniently located stores staffed by knowledgeable sales clerks. *22 Rivlin St.* ☎ *02/625-9703. Kosher & non-kosher. Map p 78; 3 Ha'armonim St., Mahane Yehuda.* ☎ *02/623-1404. AE, DC, MC, V. Map p 80.*

★★ **Winery** MAMILLA—Jerusalem's best selection of exclusively kosher wines, explained by the Mamilla Hotel's sommelier and sold at wine store prices. *11 Shlomo Hamelekh St., second floor.* ☎ *02/548-2230. Kosher. AE, DC, MC, V. Map p 78.* ●

5 The Best of the **Outdoors**

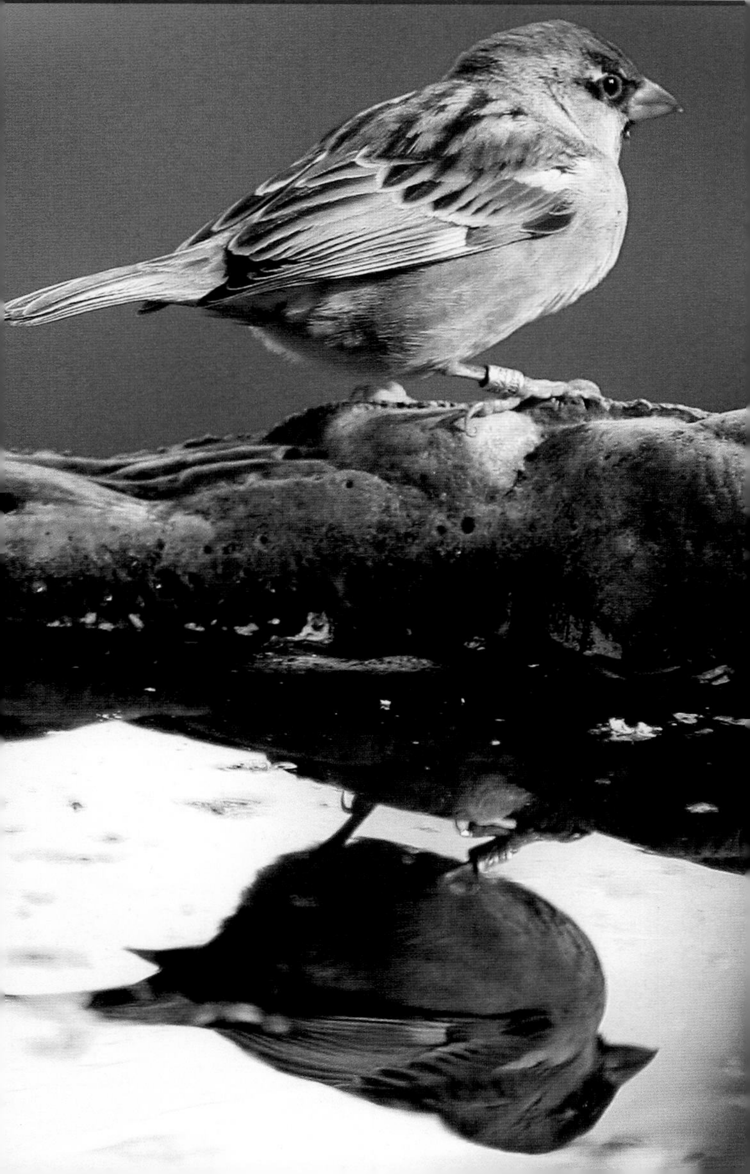

Mt. of Olives & Mt. Scopus

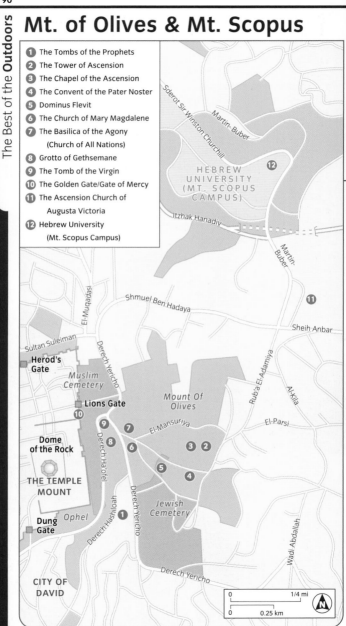

1 The Tombs of the Prophets
2 The Tower of Ascension
3 The Chapel of the Ascension
4 The Convent of the Pater Noster
5 Dominus Flevit
6 The Church of Mary Magdalene
7 The Basilica of the Agony
   (Church of All Nations)
8 Grotto of Gethsemane
9 The Tomb of the Virgin
10 The Golden Gate/Gate of Mercy
11 The Ascension Church of
   Augusta Victoria
12 Hebrew University
   (Mt. Scopus Campus)

One of the temporary residents of the Jerusalem Bird Observatory.

The theme "sacred to all three monotheistic religions" applies to the **Mount of Olives**—but what makes it great for outdoor adventure is its combination of spectacular vistas and beautiful gardens, in addition to various holy sites. It is impossible not to notice the vast Jewish cemetery, while Christians have left a legacy of six churches here. This is also where Muslims believe a drama of divine judgment will occur: A tightrope as narrow as a wire will one day stretch from the Mount of Olives to the Dome of the Rock, and all humankind will walk across the wire on the way to eternity—the righteous will reach the other side safely as the wicked fall to their deaths in the valley below. START: **The observation platform in front of the Seven Arches Hotel at the top of the Mount of Olives.**

1 ★ The Tombs of the Prophets. These tombs are ascribed to the Old Testament Prophets Haggai, Zechariah, and Malachi, who lived in the 5th century BCE. Thus, the cemetery that occupies the entire summit and slopes of the Mount of Olives has been in use from Biblical times to the present day (the Seven Arches Hotel is not only built right on top of Jewish graves, many headstones were used in its construction by the Jordanians). Because of its proximity to the Temple Mount, this is the cemetery of choice for religious Jews who came to the Holy Land to die; many believe the resurrection will begin here. ⏲ *15 min. Free admission. Sun–Fri 8am–3pm.*

2 The Tower of Ascension. The tallest structure on the Mount of Olives, it is part of a Russian Orthodox church—one of a cluster of churches of various denominations built in the vicinity where Jesus is believed to have ascended to heaven following his resurrection. The chapel contains a beautiful mosaic floor dating back to Byzantine times. No shorts for men; women must wear skirts. *Tues–Thurs 9am–noon.*

3 ★ The Chapel of the Ascension. This very ancient small church is actually now within a mosque, since Muslims also revere Jesus as a prophet. Some claim that an imprint in the stone floor is the footstep of Jesus. Ring the doorbell for admission. ⏲ *15 min. Admission NIS 5 adults. Daily during daylight hr.*

4 ★★ The Convent of the Pater Noster. This Carmelite convent is built over the ruins of a

The Tomb of the Prophets has been in use from Biblical times to the present day.

The Tower of the Ascension is the tallest structure on the Mount of Olives.

Crusader chapel constructed where Jesus was thought to have instructed his disciples in the Lord's Prayer; there is some evidence to suggest that the disciples stayed here when sojourning in Jerusalem.

Tiles along the cloister walls are inscribed with the Lord's Prayer in more than 180 languages and dialects, some no longer spoken and others not expressed in written characters anywhere else in the world. It is certainly possible that as a Jewish preacher, Jesus might have used the language of this prayer: It contains no elements of later Christian theology. 🕐 *15 min.* ☎ *02/626-4904. Mon–Sat 8:30am–noon & 2:30–4:30pm; closed Sun.*

5 ★ **Dominus Flevit.** The teardrop-shaped Dominus Flevit (which translates as "the Lord wept") is built on the spot where Jesus was said to have wept over the future destruction of Jerusalem. It is a rare example of a church that faces west, rather than east, so that it looks toward the site of the Biblical Holy of Holies in the ancient Temple. 🕐 *15 min.* ☎ *02/626-6450. Free admission. Daily 8–11:45am & 2:30–5pm.*

6 ★★ **The Church of Mary Magdalene.** This 19th-century Russian Orthodox gem, visible from afar because of its golden spires of

Majestic Views

The ridge just to the east of the Temple Mount comprising the Mount of Olives and Mount Scopus represents a significant geographic demarcation: It is the dividing line between the forested Judean Hills and the Judean Desert, which extends from the eastern edge of Jerusalem down to Jericho and the Dead Sea. It is easy to be so captivated by the view of Jerusalem that you forget to look in the opposite direction. But do not fail to look east, especially from Mount Scopus, to take in the beauty of the desert. On most days, you can see the hills of Moab across the valley of the Jordan River; on especially clear days, you can see the northern tip of the Dead Sea to the southeast. *Tip:* Visit the Mount of Olives in the morning, when the sun is behind you as you face the city; the view—the best anywhere of the Temple Mount—would be spoiled by sun in your eyes in the afternoon.

The Basilica of the Agony was built with help from 16 different countries.

onion-shaped domes topped with gilded Russian crosses, is said to contain a relic of Mary Magdalene's bones. This exquisite church of white sandstone burnished to look like marble, built in 1888 by Czar Alexander III (1845–1894), so enchanted the visiting Grand Duchess Elizabeth Feodorovna (1864–1918) that she expressed the wish to be buried here; Feodorovna, Queen Victoria's (1819–1901) granddaughter, was indeed interred here after she was brutally murdered the day after the Bolsheviks killed the Romanovs during the Russian revolution (see p 61, ❹). Also buried here is Princess Alice of Battenberg (1885–1969), the mother-in-law of Queen Elizabeth II (1926–), who is honored at Yad Vashem, as well, for her role in saving Greek Jews during the Holocaust. ⏱ *20 min.* ☎ *02/628-4371. Free admission. Tues & Thurs 10–11:30am.* See p 40, ❼.

❼ ★★★ **The Basilica of the Agony.** This Roman Catholic house of worship is also called the **Church of All Nations,** as it was built by 16 different countries. The edifice, designed by the same architect who designed Dominus Flevit, is adorned with a multi-colored, golden mosaic facade that can be seen as far away as the Haas Promenade. The altar is on a rock where Jesus supposedly prayed the night before his arrest. ⏱ *20 min.* ☎ *02/626-6444. Free admission. Daily 8am–noon; Apr–Oct daily 2–6pm, Nov–Mar daily 2–5pm.*

❽ ★★ **Grotto of Gethsemane.** This is the area where Jesus is thought to have spent his fitful night before being betrayed and imprisoned. Today, it is a beautifully tended garden amid centuries-old olive trees. ⏱ *20 min.* ☎ *02/626-6444. Free admission. Daily 8am–noon; Mon–Wed, Fri & Sat 2:30–5pm; Sun & Thurs 2:30–3:30pm.*

❾ ★★ **The Tomb of the Virgin.** This underground chamber is said to be the place where Mary's body

The Grotto of Gethsemane is where Jesus is thought to have spent his final night before imprisonment.

The Tomb of the Virgin is where the mother of Jesus is said to have lain before rising to heaven.

lay before her assumption into heaven; several holes have been bored through the wall to enable pilgrims to touch the bench where Mary's body was lain after she had fallen into eternal sleep (see p 40, ⑦). ⏱ *15 min.* ☎ *02/628-4613. Free admission. May to Oct daily 5am–noon & 2:30–5pm; Nov to Apr daily 6am–noon & 2:30–5pm.*

⑩ **The Golden Gate/Gate of Mercy.** Before taking leave of the magnificent view from the Mount of

The tower atop the Ascension Church of Augusta Victoria provides excellent views of the surrounding area.

Olives, cast a last look at the gate that is theologically the most important (to all three religions) of all Jerusalem's gates: the sealed-up gate with the double arches we see in the eastern wall of the Temple Mount. It is called the Golden Gate by Christians and the Gate of Mercy by both Jews and Muslims (although the Arabic name translates into the Gate of Eternal Life). It has been blocked ever since Sultan Suleiman (1520–1566) sealed it after defeating the Crusaders in order to prevent the Jewish Messiah from entering. *It is not possible to approach the gate.*

⑪ ★★ **The Ascension Church of Augusta Victoria.** This complex, named for the wife of Kaiser Wilhelm (1859–1941), was originally built in the early 20th century as a German Protestant house of worship and pilgrimage center. When the British conquered Jerusalem in 1917 from the Ottoman Turks and their German allies, Governor General Herbert Samuel made this compound his official residence. It now serves as a hospital for East Jerusalem's Arab residents (although many are also treated at the neighboring Hadassah Hospital on Mount Scopus). There are terrific views from the top of the squat, square

Getting There

Jerusalem's familiar green Egged buses travel to Mount Scopus but not to the Mount of Olives, which is served by the blue-and-white bus 75 that leaves from the East Jerusalem station on Sultan Suleiman Street. In order to avoid the uphill climb, most visitors take a cab to the top of the Mount of Olives and begin the gentle descent from there, stopping to visit the ancient sites. Hikers can walk all along the ridge from the Mount of Olives to Mount Scopus, where there is a choice of three options: Walk down into the valley to East Jerusalem and the Old City; walk westward past the university campus, Hadassah Hospital, and the British First World War Cemetery to Route 1; or return to West Jerusalem by bus. **Note:** Many of the Mount of Olives churches have odd or severely restricted visiting hours.

Evangelical Tower of Ascension. ⏱ *20 min.* ☎ *02/628-7044. Free admission. Mon–Sat 8:30am–1pm.*

⓬ ★★ **Hebrew University (Mt. Scopus Campus).** This campus of the Hebrew University was built after this ridge was retaken by Israel in the Six Day War of 1967. Actually, a small part of the hill remained under Israeli control all during the years 1948 to 1967; every 2 weeks, a U.N. convoy made its way past Jordanian soldiers to rotate men and supplies in that lonely outpost.

The name of the mount comes from the Greek meaning "to look out;" it is easy to see why, after taking in the views of the city and the desert from the present-day university amphitheater. As you gaze on the Temple Mount from here, imagine that you are standing right where the Roman General Titus did when he surveyed what he was about to destroy in the year 70 CE. ⏱ *20 min. Observation points at the southeastern edge of the campus as you approach from the Mount of Olives. Free admission.*

The Hebrew University amphitheater is a great lookout over the city and surrounding desert.

Ramparts Walk

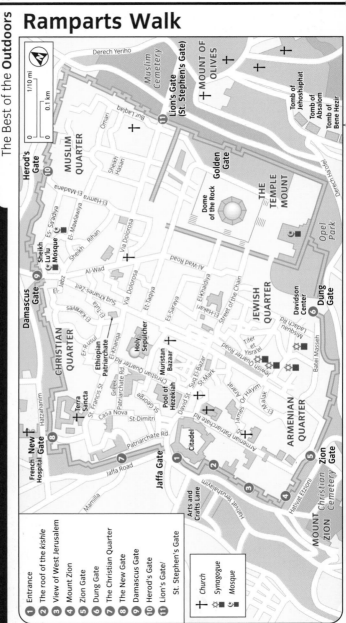

1 Entrance
2 The roof of the *kishle*
3 View of West Jerusalem
4 Mount Zion
5 Zion Gate
6 Dung Gate
7 The Christian Quarter
8 The New Gate
9 Damascus Gate
10 Herod's Gate
11 Lion's Gate/
   St. Stephen's Gate

Church
Synagogue
Mosque

It is possible to enjoy a terrific lesson on the history and geography of Jerusalem while breathing in the fresh, clean air of the Judean Hills—by walking around virtually the entire Old City atop the ancient walls that encircle it. The ticket office sells explanatory maps and books (starting at NIS 5), as well as an audio guide; together with plaques placed along the route, they make it possible to do the walk without hiring a guide (although you'd surely miss some piquant details here and there). START: **Jaffa Gate.**

❶ Entrances and logistics. For security reasons, the section of the walls closest to the Temple Mount (the easternmost wall) is not part of the walk. Thus, a complete circuit actually consists of two loops—a southern and a northern one—that do not connect. The entrance to the southern route is on the Citadel of David side of Jaffa Gate, while the entrance to the northern route is on the other side of Jaffa Gate. The southern route takes about 45 minutes and ends at Dung Gate; the northern route takes approximately 70 minutes and ends at Lion's Gate. It is possible to exit at a few of the other gates, but the entrances are only at Jaffa Gate or Damascus Gate. One should allow at least 3 hours for both, taking into account returning to Jaffa Gate and a refreshment break. In summer, it is best to start as soon as the ramparts open in the morning, before it gets too warm. Even the hardiest hikers should avoid the walk on a drizzly day: The stones get slippery when wet. **Note:** The stairways at the entrances are a bit steep; moreover, there are short up-and-down flights of very high steps every so often. *Jaffa Gate.* ☎ *02/627-7550. Admission NIS 16 adults; NIS 8 students, children & seniors. Sat–Thurs 9am–4pm, Fri 9am–2pm.*

❷ The roof of the kishle. You are standing just above the white roof of the *kishle*—Jerusalem's central prison during the four centuries of Ottoman Turkish rule. You probably previously walked right by the yard where you now see police horses grazing; you would never otherwise dream they are there. Underneath the ground on both sides of the wall are the surmised ruins of King Herod's palace, awaiting archaeological excavation (and Armenian Patriarchate permission to begin).

❸ View of West Jerusalem. The view of the New City is even more encompassing than that of the Old City: One sees clearly the southern end of City Hall/Safra Square, where the border between Israel and Jordan ran between 1948 and 1967, cutting the Holy City in half;

A view of Sultan's Pool in West Jerusalem.

Dormition Abbey on Mt. Zion.

the modern complex of Mamilla and Sultan's Pool, no-man's land during that 20-year period; and Yemin Moshe/Mishkenot Sha'ananin, the first Jewish neighborhood outside the Old City walls. On the Old City side of the wall, we can peer into the Armenian Quarter.

4 Mount Zion. The southeastern corner of the city walls affords a bird's eye view of Mount Zion, including the courtyard of Dormition Abbey and its surrounding patchwork of small cemeteries belonging to the various Christian denominations of old Jerusalem. Just west of Mount Zion is the Valley of Hinnom, the natural geographic dividing line between the east and west sides of the city. Some landmarks we can see clearly are the Cinematheque, the Menachem Begin Heritage Center, and St. Andrew's Church.

5 Zion Gate. This is the main pedestrian entrance directly into the Jewish Quarter—and the historic portal through which the Jews who survived the battles of 1948 straggled out after Israel surrendered the Old City to Jordan. Note the white dome of the rebuilt Hurva Synagogue. From our perch, we have a great reverse view of the Haas, Sherover, and Goldman promenades, from where we witness the dramatic vistas of the Old City skyline.

6 Dung Gate. This gate's unflattering name derives from the refuse

The Damascus Gate connects East Jerusalem with the Old City.

The Rockefeller Museum across from Herod's Gate.

that was dumped here in Biblical times (Nehemiah made reference to it), probably because the prevailing winds would carry odors away. Our bird's-eye view is of the Western Wall Plaza, Ophel Archaeological Park, City of David, Kidron Valley, Mount of Olives and, in the near and far distance, the Judean Desert.

7 The Christian Quarter. Our eastern view is of the section of the Old City containing its oldest churches and the Via Dolorosa; to the west, we see the impressive Pontifical Institute of Notre Dame.

8 The New Gate. Beneath us is a gate that can be called "new" only in the context of millennia of history: it is the only entrance that was not part of Jerusalem's 16th-century walls; it dates back merely to the late 19th century, when the Ottoman Empire created it in order to allow Christian pilgrims easier access to their holy places.

9 Damascus Gate. Named for the Syrian city in whose direction this imposing gate faces, this is the principal entryway connecting downtown East Jerusalem with the Old City; the never-ending parade of foot traffic bears testimony to its centrality. Within the walls, we observe the bustle of the *souk* sans the crowd and shifting scents, as well as the homes—some of them quite splendid—of the Muslim Quarter.

10 Herod's Gate. The English is a misnomer; in Arabic and Hebrew, this is called Flower Gate, possibly after the stone rosette carved above it. Across the street is the grand Rockefeller Museum; beyond it and to the right from this vantage point is Mt. Scopus.

11 Lion's Gate/St. Stephen's Gate. The name is taken from the pair of fierce felines depicted on the gate's flanks—although they are in fact meant to portray tigers, the heraldic symbol of a medieval sultan. Christians refer to it as St. Stephen's Gate, after the martyr believed to have been stoned nearby. This is the most direct entry to the Via Dolorosa, and the passage Israeli soldiers stormed when recapturing the city during the Six Day War. Take a long moment to look down into Gethsemane and up along the Mount of Olives.

Promenades, Gardens & Parks

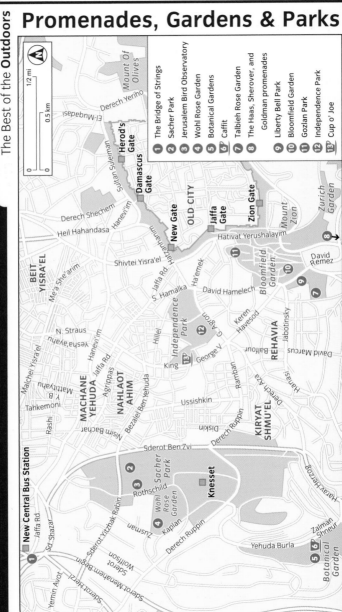

1 The Bridge of Strings
2 Sacher Park
3 Jerusalem Bird Observatory
4 Wohl Rose Garden
5 Botanical Gardens
6 Caffit
7 Talbieh Rose Garden
8 The Haas, Sherover, and Goldman promenades
9 Liberty Bell Park
10 Bloomfield Garden
11 Gozlan Park
12 Independence Park
13 Cup o' Joe

1/2 mi
0.5 km

Mount Of Olives

Derech Yeriho
El-Mugadasi

Sultan Suleiman
Herod's Gate
Damascus Gate

Derech Shechem
Heil Hahandasa   Hanevi'im

New Gate   OLD CITY

Jaffa Gate
Zion Gate

BEIT YISRA'EL   Shivtei Yisra'el   Jaffa Rd.
Mea She'arim   Hanevi'im   HaEmek
N. Straus   Hillel   Hativat Yerushalayim   Mount Zion   Zurich Garden

Malchei Yisra'el   Yesha'ayahu
Y.B. Mattityahu
Tahkemoni
Rashi   Nisim Bachar   Bezalel Ben Yehuda

MACHANE YEHUDA   Agrippas
NAHLAOT AHIM

King   George V   Keren Hayesod
Ussishkin   Ramban   Balfour   Jabotinsky

David Hamelech   Bloomfield Garden   David Remez

Independence Park   G. Agron   REHAVIA   David Marcus

KIRYAT SHMU'EL   Derech 'Aza   Hanasi

Sderot Ben Zvi   Diskin   Derech Ruppin

New Central Bus Station
Jaffa Rd.
Sd. Shazar

Sacher Park   Knesset

Wohl Rose Garden
Rothschild
Zusman   Kaplan

Sderot Yitzhak Rabin
Sderot Menachem Begin
Sderot Wolfson
Yemin Avot   Sderot Herzl

Derech Ruppin   Yehuda Burla   Zalman Shneur   Botanical Garden   HaRav Herzog

All of Jerusalem is a living museum, best observed from the outdoors. In addition, its green spaces are enjoyed year-round by the families who live here. The peaceful co-existence of the city's Muslim and Jewish inhabitants is reflected by their shared use of its parks, picnic areas, gardens, and playgrounds. START: **Jaffa Road at Herzl Blvd.**

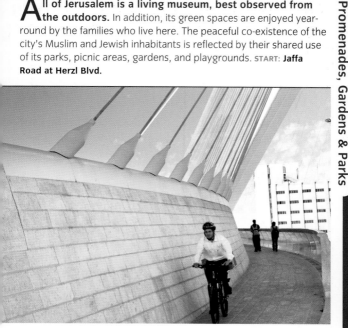

The modern Bridge of Strings was designed by world-renowned architect Santiago Calatrava.

1 ★★★ **The Bridge of Strings.** Also known as the Chords Bridge, this is Jerusalem's newest landmark, dedicated on Israel's 60th birthday in May of 2008. Designed by world-renowned architect Santiago Calatrava (1951–) and inspired by the shape of David's harp, its modernity caused controversy in a city that treasures its connections with its ancient past. It crosses the maze of intersections at the main western entrance to the city and is designed to carry trams of the light rail system (scheduled to begin running in late 2010), as well as pedestrians, who already use the bridge. *At the main (western) entrance to/exit from the city, where Jaffa Rd. intersects with Herzl Blvd.*

2 kids **Sacher Park.** This mostly flat park is the city favorite for pick-up soccer games, as well as for Israeli families who throw elaborate barbecues here, using either the few built-in pits or bringing their own portable rigs. There is a large playground, as well as bike and jogging paths (with a few work-out stations alongside) that extend across Ruppin Road into the Valley of the Cross. *The park extends along Haim Hazaz Boulevard between Gaza Road and Ruppin Road, and along Ben Zvi Boulevard between Ruppin Road and Agripas Street.*

3 kids **Jerusalem Bird Observatory.** Israel is one of the world's main migratory routes for birds seeking the warmer climes of

Sacher Park is a favorite for families.

summer in Europe and winter in Africa. In the spring (Mar–May) and fall (Sept–Nov), therefore, flocks of birds are attracted by the lawns, colors, and pond of the Wohl Rose Park; accordingly, the government set aside an acre of land abutting that park for the Jerusalem region's primary ornithology center. Visitors can watch the birds without disturbing them from inside an enclosed wooden structure. It is always advisable to check the website or call ahead to find out the best times to come during the season you are there, as well as to inquire about

The Wohl Rose Garden stretches from the Knesset to the Supreme Court.

special events; you might even be able to join scientists in applying bands (or rings) to avian passers-by for tracking purposes. ⏱ *1 hr.*
The western edge of Sacher Park, between the buildings housing the Knesset and the Supreme Court.
☎ *052/386-9488. www.jbo.org.il. Free admission. Open 24 hours a day. Phone or check the website for special event admission fees.*

④ ★ **Wohl Rose Garden.**
Stretching for 19 acres between the Knesset and the Supreme Court, the Wohl Rose Park—the largest of its kind in the Middle East—contains some 15,000 bushes representing nearly 400 varieties of roses. Its Garden of Nations is made up of sections donated from around the world. ⏱ *1 hr. Enter opposite the Knesset's Palombo Gate. Open during daylight hr.*

⑤ ★★ **kids Botanical Gardens.**
The finest botanical gardens in the country—and likely in the entire Middle East—feature more than 6,000 plant species from all over the world and especially the Mediterranean basin. The tropical greenhouse is exceptional; kids of all ages will love the butterfly house, not to mention the swans gliding on the pond. The gardens attract many birds in the early morning and evening hours; a sightseeing trackless "train" runs mid-morning to mid-afternoon. The highlight of the year

is the Orchid Festival, held during the Passover holiday; it is worth checking the website for other special events (like free Shakespeare performances) throughout the year. *Burla St., Nayot.* ☎ *02/679-4012/3. http://botanic.co.il. Admission NIS 25 adults, NIS 15 students & seniors. Tickets for Sat must be purchased in advance. Gardens Sat–Thurs 7am– sunset, Fri 7am–3pm; tropical conservatory Sun–Thurs 10am–3pm, Fri & Sat 10am–2pm; train runs Mon– Thurs 10am–2pm on the hour.*

The charming  ★ Caffit cafe, one of the chain of the same name, overlooks the Botanical Garden pond. Seating is available in the air-conditioned indoors if it is too hot to sit on the terrace. There is no charge to enter the gardens in order to go to the cafe. ☎ *02/648-0003. $$. Kosher.*

7 Talbieh Rose Garden. This is a very pleasant little garden in a quiet residential neighborhood. It contains vine-covered trellises and a giant fig tree; it also offers a nice view of southern Jerusalem. *Intersection of Dubnov & Pinsker sts.*

8 ★★★ The Haas, Sherover, and Goldman promenades. This trio of promenades affords breathtaking views of the Old City and Judean Desert. The **Haas**

Promenade (see p 14) runs east-west and forms a ninety-degree angle with the north-south **Sherover Promenade.** The **Goldman Promenade** picks up where the Haas leaves off and meanders through a lovely wooded area, conveniently dotted with picnic tables. The trails here are not paved. The Goldman Promenade enjoys the most natural shade and is best experienced in daylight; the Haas and the Sherover, which skirts a charming convent and affords the best views of the terrain of east Jerusalem descending towards the Jordan River, can also be enjoyed in the early evening. *Start at the north side of Daniel Yanovsky St., extending east from Ha'askan St.*

9 kids Liberty Bell Park. This popular park is named for its replica of the U.S.'s Liberty Bell, which it has housed since the 1976 bicentennial. It contains multiple playgrounds, a terraced pergola, basketball courts, an amphitheater, and statues of a dragon and a dinosaur for the little ones to climb. The park runs parallel to Bloomfield Garden (see p 66, **5**) on the opposite side of King David Street, but extends even further southward, where the Puppet Theatre resides (see p 54, **12**). *Corner of Jabotinsky and King David Streets.*

10 ★★ Bloomfield Garden. This stretch of green begins just west of

Swans swim in the pond of the Botanical Gardens, which has over 6,000 plant species from around the world.

Liberty Bell Park is named for its replica of the U.S. bell.

the Yemin Moshe quarter and extends south, with beautiful views of Mt. Zion and the Valley of Hinnom. The flower beds along King David Street are always decorative—especially so each spring, when they come alive with tulips. Within the garden lies an anonymous grave from the Herodian period, and at the southern end is one of the city's loveliest fountains. ⏱ *20 min. From the Yemin Moshe windmill to David Remez Sq.*

⓫ **Gozlan Park.** Set just behind the King David Hotel, this once bore the nickname "The Fragrant Orchard" for the spice trees that grew there. It is a nice place to relax while taking in a close-up view of the Old City wall. *Enter from Emile Botta St.*

⓬ ★ **Independence Park.** Jerusalem's "Central Park" is just steps from downtown—the perfect place to bring a picnic purchased in a nearby deli or snack shop. The gently sloping park also constitutes a scenic route to the new Alrov Mamilla pedestrian mall (see p 27). The lower section contains an old Muslim cemetery that was deconsecrated by the *Waqf* (Muslim Religious Authority) in order to build the Palace Hotel; this did not prevent a controversy erupting over the construction of the already-begun Museum of Tolerance (between the park and Hillel St.). ⏱ *30 min. Demarcated by Agron St., King George Ave., King David St. & Hillel St.*

⓭ **Cup o' Joe,** a pioneering chain of coffee shops that began in the 1990s in Tel Aviv, has its main Jerusalem branch at the top of the park. Its round shape and floor-to-ceiling windows make for a nice view. *41 King George St.* ☎ *02/622-1492. $$. Kosher.* ●

Guided Segway Tours

From the same folks who bring you the underground water tunnel tours (unless you take them with a private guide) comes a novel way to enjoy the city: on Segway Personal Transporters (PTs). City of David Tours (☎ *6033; http://cityofdavid.org.il) organizes tours led by professionals that take riders—equipped with the necessary safety equipment—along the Haas Promenade.

Jerusalem Dining

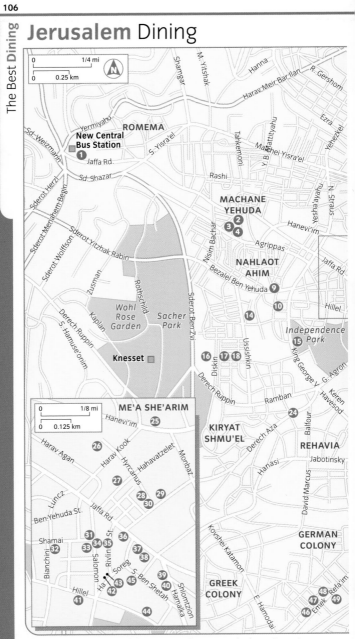

Previous page: La Guta was one of the city's first gourmet kosher restaurants.

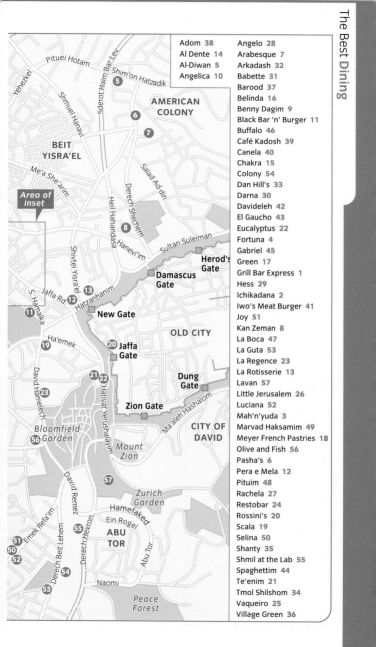

Adom 38
Al Dente 14
Al-Diwan 5
Angelica 10

Angelo 28
Arabesque 7
Arkadash 32
Babette 31
Barood 37
Belinda 16
Benny Dagim 9
Black Bar 'n' Burger 11
Buffalo 46
Café Kadosh 39
Canela 40
Chakra 15
Colony 54
Dan Hill's 33
Darna 30
Davideleh 42
El Gaucho 43
Eucalyptus 22
Fortuna 4
Gabriel 45
Green 17
Grill Bar Express 1
Hess 29
Ichikadana 2
Iwo's Meat Burger 41
Joy 51
Kan Zeman 8
La Boca 47
La Guta 53
La Regence 23
La Rotisserie 13
Lavan 57
Little Jerusalem 26
Luciana 52
Mah'n'yuda 3
Marvad Haksamim 49
Meyer French Pastries 18
Olive and Fish 56
Pasha's 6
Pera e Mela 12
Pituim 48
Rachela 27
Restobar 24
Rossini's 20
Scala 19
Selina 50
Shanty 35
Shmil at the Lab 55
Spaghettim 44
Te'enim 21
Tmol Shilshom 34
Vaqueiro 25
Village Green 36

Dining Best Bets

Hottest New Restaurant
★★★ Mah'n'yuda $$$ *10 Beit Yaakov St. (p 119)*

Best Cafe/Patisserie
★★ Meyer French Pastries $$ *22 Keren Kayemet St. (p 116)*

Best Brunch
★★★ Arabesque $$$$ *American Colony Hotel (p 109)*

Best Burger (Non-Kosher)
★ Iwo's $$ *10 Shamai St. (p 114)*

Best Burger (Kosher)
★★ Vaqueiro $$$ *54 HaNevi'im St. (p 118)*

Best American-Style Bagel
★★ Green $$ *26 Keren Kayemet St. (p 113)*

Best Deli
★★★ Hess $$$ *9 Heleni Hamalka (p 114)*

Best Fish
★★★ Shmil at the Lab $$$ *Old Railway Yard (p 118)*

Best Tasting Menu
★★★ Chakra $$$$ *41 King George St. (p 111)*

Best Shwarma
★ Arkadash $ *6 Shamai St. (p 110)*

Best Tapas
★★★ La Rotisserie $$$$ *3 Hativat Hatzanhanim (p 116)*

Best Cheesecake
★ Al Dente $$$ *50 Ussishkin St. (p 109)*

Best Biblical Culinary Experience
★★ Eucalyptus $$$ *14 Hutzot Hayotzer (p 113)*

Best Organic Vegetarian/ Vegan
★ Village Green $$ *33 Jaffa Rd. (p 118)*

Arkadash is renowned for its shwarma.

Jerusalem Dining A to Z

Anjelica has been called one of the country's 10 best restaurants.

★★★ **Adom** NAHALAT SHIVA *MEDITERRANEAN* One of West Jerusalem's best non-kosher restaurants, Adom serves seafood but not pork. Consider ordering main courses in starter portions to savor more dishes. *31 Jaffa Rd. (Feingold Courtyard).* ☎ *02/624-6242. Entrees NIS 50–NIS 130. AE, DC, MC, V. Lunch & dinner daily.*

★ **Al Dente** DOWNTOWN *ITALIAN* Just a few blocks from the Ben Yehuda pedestrian mall, this little place has the feel of a neighborhood restaurant. The pastas are made fresh, the soups are good, and the mascarpone cheesecake outstanding. *50 Ussishkin St.* ☎ *02/625-1479. Entrees NIS 38–NIS 62. Kosher. MC, V. Lunch Sun–Fri, dinner Sat–Thurs.*

kids **Al-Diwan** EAST JERUSALEM *MIDDLE EASTERN/CONTINENTAL* Located in the Ambassador Hotel in East Jerusalem's consular district, the food is unremarkable, but a reasonable choice when children want familiar dishes while the adults wish to try local fare. *Entrance at 4 Antara Ben-Shadad St.* ☎ *02/541-2222.*

Entrees NIS 40–NIS 80. AE, DC, MC, V. Lunch & dinner daily.

★★★ **Angelica** DOWNTOWN *CONTINENTAL/GRILL* The favorite restaurant of Israel's foreign minister, when he is dining alone or in the company of visiting foreign dignitaries. Angelica has been praised as one of the country's 10 best restaurants by the leading national daily newspaper, *Haaretz. 7 Shatz St. (at the Montefiore Hotel).* ☎ *02/623-0056. Entrees NIS 65–NIS 140. Kosher. AE, DC, MC, V. Lunch Sun–Thurs, dinner Sat–Thurs.*

★★ **Angelo** DOWNTOWN *ITALIAN* Owner Angelo is a Roman native whose fresh pasta—also available in optional whole wheat—is excellent; gnocchi fans will especially be pleased. Sublime tiramisu, authentic espresso. *9 Hyrkanos St.* ☎ *02/623-6095. Entrees NIS 48–NIS 85. Kosher (no meat). AE, DC, MC, V. Dinner Sat–Thurs.*

★★★ **Arabesque** EAST JERUSALEM *MIDDLE EASTERN/CONTINENTAL* The dining room of this legendary hotel serves an equally celebrated Saturday brunch and

Saving Money With "Business" Lunches

Most restaurants in West Jerusalem—from the least expensive to the most exclusive—offer "business meals" at reduced prices. This meal will generally comprise two courses (including one main course) and a drink. Most offers extend between noon and 5pm, some until 6pm, and even the rare 7pm (more of an "early bird" dinner special than lunch). Some chains (Rahmo, Iwo's) advertise "business meals" all day long—but only the Hebrew menu might alert you to this fact. In addition, coupons are available in two useful publications found in most hotel lobbies: *Jerusalem Menus* and *Jerusalem Coupons* (www.jerusalem-coupons.com).

high tea every afternoon, best enjoyed in the naturally shaded courtyard. *American Colony Hotel, 2 Louis Vincent St. (corner of Nablus Rd.).* ☎ *02/627-9777. Brunch NIS 160, entrees NIS 90–NIS 160. AE, DC, MC, V. Brunch Sat, lunch Sun–Fri, dinner daily.*

Arkadash DOWNTOWN *GRILL*
The three vertical spits at Arkadash yield up mouthwatering turkey, lamb, or veal *shwarma*; the house specialty combines all three. The kebab is also superb. *Shamai St., at the corner of the passage across from McDonalds. No phone. NIS 12–NIS 35. Kosher. AE, MC, V. Lunch Sun–Fri, dinner daily.*

Babette DOWNTOWN *WAFFLES*
Babette is an institution in Jerusalem and can be credited with popularizing Belgian waffles in the city; most ice cream parlors now offer waffles a la mode. Babette is still a hole-in-the wall, so waiting in line is part of the experience. The waffle itself is quite thick, perhaps at the expense of a crunchier crust. *16 Shamai St.* ☎ *02/625-7004. NIS 20–NIS 25. Kosher. No credit cards. Lunch Sun–Thurs, dinner daily.*

★★★ **Barood** NAHALAT SHIVA *MEDITERRANEAN*   Barood offers creative cocktails and eclectic food—from American barbeque to Sephardic specialties—prepared with pride and authenticity. *31 Jaffa Rd. (Feingold Courtyard).* ☎ *02/625-9081. Entrees NIS 40–NIS 90. AE, MC, V. Lunch Sun–Fri, dinner Sun–Thurs, late night Sat–Thurs.*

★ **Belinda** REHAVIA *VEGETARIAN*
Belinda's successful cafe shifted to this upscale neighborhood during the intifada; her loyal customers from downtown still come for the scones and pies (some with "no sugar added"), or on a chilly day, a bowl of thick soup. *9 Diskin St.* ☎ *02/563-3995. Entrees NIS 35–NIS 55. Kosher. AE, MC, V. Sun–Thurs breakfast, lunch, and dinner; Fri breakfast and lunch.*

★ **Benny Dagim** DOWNTOWN *FISH*   Jerusalemites who know fish have been coming here for 38 years. Fish are prepared in multiple tempting ways; a favorite is a whole St. Peter's fish from the Sea of Galilee. *1 Mesilat Yesharim St.* ☎ *02/625-2403. Entrees NIS 45–NIS 75. Kosher. AE, DC, MC, V. Lunch Sun–Thurs, dinner Sat–Thurs.*

Darna serves authentic Moroccan food in an exquisite setting.

★ **Black Bar 'n' Burger** DOWN-TOWN *HAMBURGERS* The only kosher branch of this popular national chain, Black features an extensive menu of flavorful hamburgers in a nightclub-like setting. A good choice if you want to wash down your burger with something fancier than a cold beer. *18 Shlomzion Hamalka St.* ☎ *02/624-6767. Entrees NIS 30–NIS 60. AE, DC, MC, V. Lunch Sun–Fri, dinner Sat–Thurs.*

★★ **Buffalo** GERMAN COLONY *STEAKHOUSE* An old-fashioned meat-and-potatoes place, with prime cuts of beef on display near the entrance. Cravings for American favorites like buffalo wings and onion rings generously satisfied. *54 Emek Refaim* ☎ *02/561-1325. Entrees NIS 65–NIS 129. AE, DC, MC, V. Lunch Sun–Thurs, dinner Sat–Thurs.*

★ **Café Kadosh** DOWNTOWN *CAFE* A quintessential Jerusalem cafe: always crowded and animated, and serving good coffee, fresh-baked pastries, and honest food. *6 Shlomzion Hamalka St.* ☎ *02/625-4210. Entrees NIS 30–NIS 60. Kosher. MC, V. Breakfast & lunch Sun–Fri, dinner daily.*

★★★ **Canela** DOWNTOWN *CONTI-NENTAL* Chef Lior Hafzadi creates delicious appetizers; stick to the meat entrees, rather than the fish. Leave room for dessert and watch the wine prices. *8 Shlomzion Hamalka St.* ☎ *02/622-2293. Entrees NIS 65–NIS 170. Kosher. AE, DC, MC, V. Lunch Sun–Thurs, dinner Sat–Thurs.*

★★★ **Chakra** DOWNTOWN *MEDI-TERRANEAN* Chef Ilan Garoussi shops personally at the market each morning: Whatever is freshest dictates that day's menu. Unique is a daily, seemingly never-ending tasting menu. *41 King George St.* ☎ *02/625-2733. Entrees NIS 50–NIS 150. AE, DC, MC, V. Brunch Sat, lunch Sun–Fri, dinner daily.*

★★ **Colony** GERMAN COLONY *MEDITERRANEAN* One of the hottest places in town, especially on Friday night. Managed by the same team that runs Adom, it draws an upscale crowd to its elegant bar. *7 Beit Lehem Rd.* ☎ *02/672-9955. Entrees NIS 48–NIS 125. AE, DC, MC, V. Lunch & dinner daily.*

★★ **Dan Hill's** NAHALAT SHIVA *PIZZA/PASTA* This is the place to go if you like cheese: Most dishes are slathered in molten yellow-and-white, and it has arguably the best kosher pizza in town. Or just come in for an old-fashioned banana split.

At Eucalyptus dishes are made from local ingredients mentioned in the Bible.

Harmony Hotel Arcade, 6 Yoel Salomon St. ☎ 02/624-2999. *Entrees NIS 40–NIS 80. Kosher. AE, DC, MC, V. Lunch Sun–Fri, dinner Sat–Thurs.*

★★★ **Darna** DOWNTOWN *MORROCAN* Dining here is like eating in an exquisite North African museum; the beauty extends to the authentic Moroccan serving dishes and waitresses' dresses. A must-try experience for people unfamiliar with this glorious cuisine. *3 Hyrcanos St.* ☎ 02/624-5406. *Entrees NIS 100–NIS 190. Kosher. AE, DC, MC, V. Lunch Sun–Thurs, dinner Sat–Thurs.*

Davideleh NAHALAT SHIVA *ISRAELI* This new Jerusalem entry has taken over one of the most coveted restaurant spots in the city; it has gotten off to a promising start. Great al fresco seating and people-watching. *7 Rivlin St.* ☎ 02/624-6316. *Entrees NIS 32–NIS 58. Kosher. MC, V. Breakfast Sun–Fri, brunch Fri, lunch Sun–Thurs, dinner Sat–Thurs.*

★★ **El Gaucho** NAHALAT SHIVA *GRILL* As the name suggests, the restaurant evokes the pampas of Argentina and its patrimony of superb beef. The longevity of this nationwide chain is testament to the popularity of its steaks. *22 Rivlin St.* ☎ 02/624-2227. *Entrees NIS 59–NIS 129. Kosher. AE, DC, MC, V. Lunch Sun–Thurs, dinner Sat–Thurs.*

★★★ **Eucalyptus** MAMILLA *BIBLICAL* Chef Moshe Basson is the acknowledged father of the cuisine of ancient Israel: Dishes are made from the ingredients of the Holy Land mentioned in the Bible—and the results are heavenly. Don't miss the signature stuffed figs. *14 Hativat Yerushalim, in the Hutzot Hayotzer artists' complex.* ☎ 02/624-4331. *Entrees NIS 39–NIS 68. Kosher. AE, DC, MC, V. Lunch Sun–Fri, dinner Sat–Thurs.*

★★ **Fortuna** MAHANE YEHUDA *GRILL* Probably the best of the popularly priced grilled meat restaurants for which the market area is famous. The meats are grilled over charcoal, and the salads are prepared freshly several times a day by the professionally trained chef. *2 Ha'armonim St.* ☎ 02/560-1787. *Entrees NIS 22–NIS 95. Kosher. AE, DC, MC, V. Lunch & dinner Sun–Thurs; summer lunch Fri, winter dinner Sat.*

★★★ **Gabriel** DOWNTOWN *FRENCH FUSION* Anyone harboring any doubt that kosher and gourmet can go together need only eat here. The restaurant works magic with foie gras; the service is impeccable. *7 Shimon ben Shetah St.* ☎ 02/624-6444. *Entrees NIS 94–NIS 175. Kosher. AE, DC, MC, V. Lunch Sun–Thurs, dinner Sat–Thurs.*

Glossary of Street Food

Burekas—These savory pastries of phyllo dough stuffed with spinach, potato, and/or white cheeses also come in miniatures and coated in sesame seeds. Many coffee shops offer a breakfast combination of burekas and hard-boiled egg.

Falafel—Chickpeas ground into a spicy paste, rolled into balls, and deep fried. Served in pita bread stuffed with accompanying salads.

Sabih—The traditional Iraqi-Jewish Sabbath dish of eggplant and hard-boiled eggs has been transformed into a popular snack: Slices of fried eggplant and cooked egg are stuffed into a pita with "chips" (aka french fries) and condiments.

Sahleb—This thick, hot beverage made from orchid root and garnished with cinnamon and ground walnuts is a winter favorite.

Shakshuka—This Tripolitan import is a spicier version of the Eastern European *lecho,* a stewed concoction of poached eggs, tomatoes, and peppers.

Shwarma—The Israeli version of Turkey's *doner* kebab—slabs of spiced meat rotating on vertical spits—has been enhanced to include varieties from lamb, veal, and/or turkey.

Falafels are a popular street food.

★ **Green** REHAVIA *VEGETARIAN* Probably the best vegetarian restaurant in Jerusalem that does not serve hot food (except for soup in winter); it's doubtful you'd find fresher ingredients anywhere. Picnics expertly packed. *26 Keren Kayemet St.* ☎ *02/563-5680. Entrees NIS 25–NIS 45. Kosher. AE, MC, V. Breakfast & lunch Sun–Fri, dinner Sun–Thurs.*

Grill Bar Express JAFFA RD. *GRILL* Just up the road from the Central Bus Station, this is a much better place to grab a quick bite than any of the forgettable joints in the station itself. It serves up an admirable *"me'urav yerushalmi"*— Jerusalem mixed grill—a tasty assortment of cuts of meat best left unspecified. *212 Jaffa Rd.* ☎ *077/885-7779. Entrees NIS 18–NIS 35.*

Kosher. No credit cards. Lunch & dinner Sun–Thurs.

★★★ **Hess** DOWNTOWN *DELI*
Marcel Hess is the undisputed king of kosher delicatessen in Jerusalem. Sandwiches are thick, the megaburgers lean, the prime steaks aged; take cold cuts with you for a future picnic. *9 Heleni Hamalka St. ☎ 02/625-5515. www.hess-restaurants.com. Entrees NIS 27–NIS 110. Kosher. AE, DC, MC, V. Dinner Sun–Thurs.*

★ **Ichikadana** MAHANE YEHUDA *INDIAN/VEGETARIAN* Tasty, authentic South Indian cuisine—a rarity in this country—in a place that might be just a tad too tiny. The value, however, is unbeatable. *4 Haeshkol St. ☎ 050/224-7070. Entrees NIS 22–NIS 40. Kosher. No credit cards. Breakfast Fri, lunch Mon–Fri, dinner Mon–Thurs.*

★★ **Iwo's Meat Burger** DOWNTOWN & GERMAN COLONY *HAMBURGERS* The owner also owns Iwo's Delicatessen (see p 84); the hamburgers reflect butcher-shop quality. Possibly Jerusalem's best cheeseburger. *28 Hillel St./38 Emek Refaim St. ☎ 02/622-2513. Entrees*

Fortuna has quality fresh salads along with its grilled meats.

NIS 28–NIS 44. AE, MC, V. Daily lunch and dinner (open late).

★★ **Joy** GERMAN COLONY *MEAT* Run by the same folks who bring you Luciana (see p 115), Joy features excellent cuisine, attentive service, and a reasonably priced wine list. *22 Emek Refaim St. ☎ 02/563-0033. Entrees NIS 65–NIS 129. Kosher. AE, DC, MC, V. Breakfast & lunch Sun–Fri, dinner Sat–Thurs.*

★★ **Kan Zeman** EAST JERUSALEM *MIDDLE EASTERN* The outdoor restaurant (heated in winter) of the Jerusalem Hotel serves up classic Arabic fare, with fresh *mezze* (assorted Oriental salads) and grilled, skewered meats. Authentic live music is performed on Mondays and Fridays. *Nablus Rd. (entrance at 4 Antara Ben-Shadad St.) ☎ 02/628-3282. www.jrshotel.com. NIS 40–NIS 85. AE, DC, MC, V. Lunch & dinner daily.*

★ **La Boca** GERMAN COLONY *LATIN* An Argentinean restaurant that is not exclusively focused on steak. Two pleasant patios (one enclosed) overlook the bustling street. *46 Emek Refaim St. ☎ 02/563-5577. Entrees NIS 47–NIS 95. Kosher. AE, DC, MC, V. Lunch Sun–Fri, dinner Sat–Thurs.*

★★★ **La Guta** GERMAN COLONY *FRENCH* One of the first truly gourmet kosher restaurants in the capital, La Guta outgrew its downtown location and now serves its elegant cuisine in a beautifully restored building. It has a lovely bar area, as well. *3 Bet Lehem Rd. ☎ 02/623-2322. Entrees NIS 80–NIS 155. Kosher. AE, DC, MC, V. Lunch Sun–Fri, dinner Sat–Thurs.*

★★★ **La Regence** KING DAVID ST. *CONTINENTAL* Chef David Biton is another young star making his mark at the signature restaurant of arguably Jerusalem's classiest hotel. A good choice for a splurge. *23 King David St. ☎ 02/620-8888. Entrees*

Hess is an outstanding kosher downtown deli.

NIS 90–NIS 215. AE, DC, MC, V. Lunch & dinner Sun–Thurs.

★ **La Rotisserie** NEW GATE *MEDITERRANEAN* Spanish Chef Rodrigo Diaz is elevating this restaurant, situated in the most elegant of surroundings, to the heights it once enjoyed in the 1980s. Saturday night features a menu of authentic *tapas. 3 Hativat Hatzanhanim (on the grounds of the Pontifical Institute of Notre Dame).* ☎ *02/627-9114. www.notredamecenter.org. Entrees $22–$50. AE, MC, DC, V. Lunch & dinner daily.*

★★ **Lavan** HEBRON RD. *ITALIAN* This is an Italian restaurant that emphasizes the Mediterranean aspect of that country's cuisine. The fantastic view adds to the enjoyment of a quality meal here. *Cinematheque, 11 Hebron Rd.* ☎ *02/673-7393. NIS 35–NIS 135. AE, DC, MC, V. Lunch & dinner daily.*

★ **kids Little Jerusalem** DOWNTOWN *CAFE/RESTAURANT* A longtime Jerusalem favorite for its tranquil location in the heart of the city, the restaurant offers special menus for children and senior citizens. The portions are huge. *Ticho*

House, 9 Abraham Ticho St. ☎ *02/624-4186. NIS 25–NIS 88. Kosher. AE, DC, MC, V. Lunch Sun–Fri, dinner Sat–Thurs; restaurant may not open Sat night if weather is inclement.*

★★★ **Luciana** GERMAN COLONY *ITALIAN* Boasting one of the city's greatest patios for al fresco dining, Luciana is also popular for its breakfasts—served until 4pm. Probably the best non-meat restaurant in this neighborhood known for its eateries. *27 Emek Refaim St.* ☎ *02/563-0111. Entrees NIS 48–NIS 97. Kosher. AE, MC, DC, V. Lunch Sun–Fri, dinner Sat–Thurs.*

★★★ **Mah'n'yuda** MAHANE YEHUDA *MEAT & SEAFOOD* This dazzling new entry burst onto the Jerusalem culinary scene with little fanfare but quickly became the "in" place to eat. The menu is a piece of paper photocopied twice daily as the menu is updated. *10 Beit Yaakov St.* ☎ *02/533-3442. Entrees NIS 48–NIS 175. AE, MC, V. Lunch & dinner daily.*

★ **Marvad Haksamim** GERMAN COLONY *YEMENITE* Yemenite restaurants have just about disappeared

Lavan offers spectacular views with its Mediterranean Italian cuisine.

in Jerusalem; even here, only three authentic ethnic dishes are on the menu. On the whole, it is a reasonable place for typical Israeli grilled meats. *42 Emek Refaim St.* ☎ *02/567-0007. Entrees NIS 48–NIS 110. Kosher. AE, MC, V. Lunch Sun–Fri, dinner Sun–Thurs.*

★★ Meyer French Pastries
REHAVIA *CAFE* Perhaps the best croissants in town, certainly the most authentic Parisian quiches and sweet tarts. Meyer mixes his own special coffee blend. *22 Keren Kay-emet St.* ☎ *02/566-1396. Entrees NIS 28–NIS 58. Kosher. AE, MC, V. Breakfast & lunch Sun–Fri.*

★ Olive and Fish LIBERTY BELL
PARK *FISH* Although this restaurant specializes in fish—and does a creditable job—the staff recommends the duck, and there are plenty of meat choices. *2 Jabotinsky St.* ☎ *02/566-5020. Entrees NIS 42–NIS 98. Kosher. AE, DC, MC, V. Lunch Sun–Thurs, dinner Sat–Thurs.*

★★ Pasha's EAST JERUSALEM
MIDDLE EASTERN Gracious service in a beautiful outdoor setting. The *mezze* (assorted Oriental salads) include a superb coarse *musabha* hummus; if available for dessert, *katayeff* (stuffed pancake) is a nice change of pace from the typically dense Arabic pastries. *13 Shimon Hatzadik St.* ☎ *02/582-5162. Entrees NIS 38–NIS 77. AE, DC, MC, V. Lunch & dinner daily.*

★★ Pera e Mela DOWNTOWN
ITALIAN Chef Gionatan Ottolenghi, one of the first Italians to open a restaurant in Jerusalem, still cuts his fettucine freshly for each dish; try the pasta with salsa *rosa,* the rich risotto, or gluten-free polenta. *6 Safra Sq.* ☎ *02/623-0280. Entrees NIS 36–NIS 58. Kosher. AE, MC, V. Lunch Sun–Thurs, dinner Sat–Thurs.*

kids Pituim GERMAN COLONY
ISRAELI Pituim has a children's menu that can be colored in; the restaurant will even provide crayons. Adults can enjoy pasta, fish, and desserts (the pastries are popular as take-out items). *5 Rachel Immenu St.* ☎ *02/566-2899. Entrees NIS 42–NIS 67. Kosher. AE, MC, V. Breakfast & lunch Sun–Fri, dinner Sat–Thurs.*

★★ Rachela DOWNTOWN *CONTINENTAL*
For a simple meal flawlessly prepared and tastefully served, try this little gem just minutes from bustling downtown: The cozy garden patio is an oasis of tranquility. *5 Hahavatzelet St.* ☎ *02/624-5613. Entrees NIS 32–NIS 55. Kosher. AE, MC, V. Breakfast & lunch Sun–Fri, dinner Sat–Thurs.*

★★★ Restobar REHAVIA *GRILL*
Very aptly named, the restaurant morphs more into a bar later it gets at night. Excellent food, creative cocktails, and good service. Pleasant al fresco dining in good weather, a cozy fireplace when it's chilly. *1 Ben Maimon St.* ☎ *02/566-5126. Entrees*

Understanding Kosher

Jewish dietary laws forbid the consumption of certain animals (such as pigs) and seafood (unless the fish has fins and scales)—even the flesh of kosher animals and fowl that have not been ritually slaughtered. More to the point for our purposes, the consumption of meat and dairy products at the same meal is also forbidden; thus, no kosher restaurant in Jerusalem that serves meat or fowl would serve milk in any form (cheese, ice cream, etc.). Finally, in order for a restaurant to be certified kosher by the rabbinic authorities, it must be closed during the Sabbath—from sundown Friday until sundown Saturday. This results in differing schedules between summer and winter, and often very late dinner hours in the summer.

NIS 33–NIS 60. AE, DC, MC, V. Breakfast, lunch & dinner daily.

★ **Rossini's** OLD CITY *CONTINENTAL* Chef Joseph Asfour, who was invited to cook for Pope Benedict XVI (1927–) during his pilgrimage, serves French and Italian fare with a nod to Arabic seasonings. The sleek, elegant decor—and full bar—are remarkable for the Old City. *32 Latin Patriarchate Rd.* ☎ *050/524-6510. Entrees NIS 45–NIS 110. AE, MC, V. Lunch & dinner Mon–Sat.*

★★ **Scala** KING DAVID ST. *MEDITERRANEAN* Chef Oren Yerushalmi's excellent appetizers and desserts outshine the entrees, which are entirely satisfactory. The bar is rather limited. *7 King David St. (in the David Citadel Hotel).* ☎ *02/620-2030. Entrees NIS 52–NIS 104. Kosher. AE, DC, MC, V. Lunch & dinner Sun-Thur, dinner Sat., closed Fri.*

★★ **Selina** GERMAN COLONY *GRILL* A very small place (especially for this neighborhood) with good food and an inventive bar. Service can be sketchy; the English-language menu is good for a few laughs. *24 Emek Refaim St.* ☎ *02/567-1947. Entrees NIS 69–NIS 125. Kosher. AE, MC, V. Lunch Sun–Fri, dinner Sat–Thurs.*

★★ **Shanty** NAHALAT SHIVA *BAR RESTAURANT* The word "mellow" was coined with this place in mind: cozy atmosphere, great bar, excellent background music, and good food. The dessert crepes topped with mounds of whipped cream are a feast for the eyes, as well as the palate. *4 Nahalat Shiva.* ☎ *02/624-3434. Entrees NIS 48–NIS 90. AE, DC, MC, V. Dinner daily.*

The cozy garden patio at Rachela.

★★★ **Shmil at the Lab** RAILYARD *JEWISH* Legendary caterer and food historian Shmil Holland draws from Jewish European and Mediterranean cuisine to prepare each dish freshly. *Old Railway Yard, 28 Hebron Rd.* ☎ *02/673-1629. Entrees NIS 35–NIS 85. Kosher. AE, DC, MC, V. Breakfast Sun–Fri, brunch Fri, lunch & dinner Sun–Thurs.*

★★ kids **Spaghettim** DOWNTOWN *ITALIAN* This eatery boasts pastas with more than 50 sauces; the food is sophisticated enough for adult tastes while still appealing to children, for whom there is a special low-cost menu. *35 Hillel St.* ☎ *02/623-5547. Entrees NIS 39–NIS 70. AE, DC, MC, V. Lunch & dinner daily.*

★★ **Te'enim** GOZLAN PARK *VEGETARIAN* The city's best purely vegetarian fare, prepared with French flair by veteran Jerusalem restaurateur Patrick Melki. The premises—and view—are stunning. *12 Emile Botta St.* ☎ *02/625-1967. Entrees NIS 39–NIS 54. AE, DC, MC, V. Lunch Sun–Fri, dinner Sun–Thurs.*

★★ **Tmol Shilshom** NAHALAT SHIVA *CAFE/RESTAURANT* A unique bookstore-cafe-restaurant with an atmosphere where both Orthodox Jews and gays can feel equally comfortable. Great salads and excellent home-baked bread. *5 Yoel Salomon St. (enter via alley at #11, to end of courtyard on left).* ☎ *02/623-2758. Entrees NIS 42–NIS 79. Kosher. AE, DC, MC, V. Breakfast & lunch Sun–Fri, dinner Sat–Thurs.*

★★★ **Vaqueiro** DOWNTOWN *GRILL* South African grillmaster Stanley Hoffman presides over the spits here. Bring your appetite: The beef, veal, turkey, and chicken wings keep on coming until you cry "uncle." But save room for the chocolate "volcano." *54 HaNevi'im St.* ☎ *02/624-7432. Entrees NIS 55–NIS 149. Dinner Sun–Thurs.*

★ kids **Village Green** DOWNTOWN *VEGETARIAN* Probably Jerusalem's most popular vegetarian restaurant; very crowded at mealtimes. Wholesome food—organic, whenever possible, and good vegan choices—served up cafeteria-style. Outdoor seating on the city's main drag. *33 Jaffa Rd.* ☎ *02/625-3065. Entrees NIS 18–NIS 43 (some priced by weight). Kosher. AE, DC, MC, V. Breakfast & lunch Sun–Fri, dinner Sun–Thurs.* ●

Shanty pairs mellow atmosphere with good food.

West Jerusalem Arts & Nightlife

Al Hakawati Palestinian
    National Theater 3
Avram Bar Café 6
Bible Lands Museum 10
Bolinat 23
Borderline 1
Brigham Young University
    Jerusalem Center 2
Bulghourji Lounge
    and Gardens 12
Holocaust Art Museum 5
Jerusalem Artists House 7

The Jerusalem Center for the
    Performing Arts 14
The Jerusalem
    Cinematheque 22
Jerusalem Symphony
    Orchestra 15
The Jerusalem YMCA 11
The Khan Theatre 19
L.A. Mayer Memorial Museum
    for Islamic Art 16
Mia Bar 27
Mirror Bar 8

Museum on the Seam 4
Semadar Theater 20
Sir Isaac and Lady Edith
    Wolfson Museum 9
Stardust 24
Sultan's Pool 13
Targ Music Center 17
The Train Puppet Theatre 18
The U. Nahon Museum of
    Italian Jewish Art 26
Yellow Submarine 21
Zolli's/Nadin 25

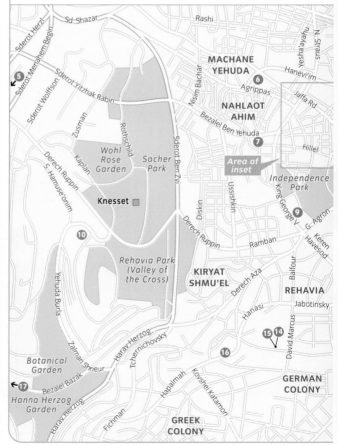

Previous page: A performance by the Jerusalem Symphony Orchestra.

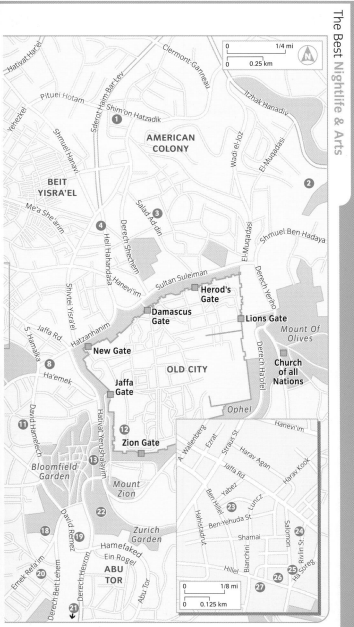

0   1/4 mi

0   0.25 km

Hativat Har'el

Pituei Hotam

Clermont-Ganneau

Itzhak Hanadiv

Yehezkel

Shmuel Hanavi

Shim'on Hatzadik **1**

AMERICAN
COLONY

Wadi el-Joz

El-Muqadasi

2

BEIT
YISRA'EL

Me'a She'arim

Salad Ad-din

3

Shmuel Ben Hadaya

Derech Shechem

4

Heil Hahandasa

Hanevi'im

El-Muqadasi

Sultan Suleiman

Herod's
Gate

Damascus
Gate

Lions Gate

Derech Yericho

Shivtei Yisra'el

Jaffa Rd.

Hatzanhanim

New Gate

OLD CITY

Derech Ha'ofel

Mount Of
Olives

S. Hamalka

8

Ha'emek

Jaffa
Gate

Church
of all
Nations

David Hamelech

11

Ophel

Hanevi'im

12

Zion Gate

A. Wallenberg

Ezrat

Straus St.

Harav Agan

13

Bloomfield
Garden

Hativat Yerushalayim

Mount
Zion

Jaffa Rd

Yabez

Luncz

Harav Kook

22

Ben Hillel

23

18

David Remez

19

Zurich
Garden

Hahistadrut

Ben-Yehuda St.

Salomon

24

Hamefaked
Ein Rogel

Shamai

Rivlin St.

20

Emek Refa'im

Derech Hevron

ABU
TOR

Abu Tor

Bianchini

Hillel

25

21

Derech Beit Lehem

Ha Soreg

26

27

0   1/8 mi

0   0.125 km

Nightlife & Performing Arts
Best Bets

Best Place for Art That Moves You
★★★ Holocaust Art Museum *Mt. of Remembrance (p 125)*

Best Place to Catch a Movie
★★★ Jerusalem Cinematheque *11 Hebron Rd. (p 127)*

Best Place for Concerts Under the Stars
★★ Sultan's Pool *Hebron Rd. at the Jaffa Gate (p 125)*

Best Upscale Bar
★★ Mirror Bar, Mamilla Hotel *11 Shlomo Hamelekh St. (p 128)*

Best Acoustics (Symphonic Concerts)
★★ Henry Crown Symphony Hall *20 Marcus St. (p 123)*

Best Ethnic Art
★★ L.A. Mayer Memorial Museum for Islamic Art *2 HaPalmach St. (p 126)*

Best Late-Night Sweet-Tooth Fix
Babette *18 Shammai St. (p 110)*

Best Place to Smoke a Nargila (Hookah)
★★ Borderline *13 Shimon Hatzadik St. (p 127)*

Best Bar in the Old City
★★ Bulghourji Lounge and Gardens *6 Armenian Patriarchate Rd. (p 128)*

Best Happy Hour
★★ Stardust *6 Rivlin St. (p 126)*

Best Bartenders
★★ Mia *18 Hillel St. (p 128)*

The Jerusalem Symphony Orchestra takes advantage of Henry Crown Hall's excellent acoustics.

Jerusalem Nightlife & Arts A to Z

The Jerusalem Center for the Performing Arts hosts more than 150 classical music performances each year.

Performance Venues (Concerts & Theater)

Al Hakawati Palestinian National Theatre
EAST JERUSALEM   The PNT performs in a variety of modes, from plays to cabaret-style productions to puppet theater. The content is often strongly political. From time to time, a specific production may be censored or unexpectedly shut down by the authorities, but both Israeli and foreign visitors are welcome; English synopses are usually available. For those interested in the Palestinian movement, a visit here can be interesting, regardless of what is being performed. *Nuzha St. (off Salaheddin St.)* ☎ *02/628-0957. Tickets NIS 25.*

★ Bible Lands Museum
MUSEUM ROW   One or two Saturday nights a month, the museum hosts concerts of solo performers or small ensembles. Wine and cheese (included with admission) is served during intermission. *25 Granot St.* ☎ *02/561-1066. www.blmj.org/en/concerts.php. Tickets NIS 65–NIS 75; discounts for students & seniors.*

★ Brigham Young University Jerusalem Center
MOUNT SCOPUS   The Middle East campus for the famed Mormon university hosts weekly classical music concerts every Sunday evening at 8pm, as well as jazz performances once a month on a Thursday evening. Tickets are free, but they must be reserved in advance. *Located on Mount Scopus, near Augusta Victoria Hospital.* ☎ *02/626-5621. www.ce.byu.edu/jc. Free admission.*

★★★ The Jerusalem Center for the Performing Arts
TALBIEH   Better known simply as the Jerusalem Theatre, there is generally something happening every night of the week in at least one of the four auditoriums. It is host to more than 150 classical music

A performance at The Train Puppet Theatre.

concerts alone each year. Major theatrical productions screen LCD subtitles (English translations above the action on the stage). *20 Marcus St., corner of Chopin St.* ☎ *02/560-5755. www.jerusalem-theatre.co.il. Performances can vary from free to hundreds of shekels.*

★★ **The Jerusalem YMCA** KING DAVID ST.   This classic building's small auditorium is a popular venue for recitals and concerts of chamber, baroque, and sacred music. The Y's Mary Nathaniel Golden Hall of Friendship is the resident venue for the Jerusalem Music Center's annual concert season. *26 King David St.* ☎ *02/569-2692. www.ymca3arch. co.il. Jerusalem Music Center box office* ☎ *02/624-1041. www.jmc.co.il. Tickets NIS 110–NIS 130.*

★ **The Khan Theatre** OLD RAILWAY STATION   Opposite the old train station is this restored khan—a roadside inn for caravans—that has been transformed into a theater. Some plays have English subtitles. *2 David Remez Sq.* ☎ *02/671-8281. www.khan.co.il. Tickets NIS 50–NIS 150.*

★★ **Sultan's Pool** JAFFA GATE   Only the biggest names perform here, so whether it is a rock concert or a visiting opera company from Italy, you will hear about it. *In a valley beneath the Old City walls between Jaffa Gate and Mount Zion.*

Classical Music

In the last 20 years or so, Israel has witnessed a massive influx of immigrants from the former Soviet Union, including many excellent musicians who have had a tremendous impact on the classical music scene in Israel, both in terms of quality and quantity: Not only did the highly regarded Israel Philharmonic Orchestra, and the Jerusalem and Tel Aviv Symphony Orchestras welcome the new additions, but even smaller cities who could never before support orchestras now found themselves with an embarrassment of riches. If you should see notices for the symphony orchestras of Rishon LeZion or Beersheba, for example, know that the high caliber of their talent is vastly disproportionate to the size of the sponsoring city.

Ticket Agencies

A good way both to find out what is going on during your stay, as well as to secure the best seats, is to visit the offices of the two major ticket agencies in town. They are conveniently located downtown and within steps of one another. **Klaim** is at 12 Shamai St. (☎ 02/622-2333; www.klaimonline.co.il). Look for **Bimot** at 8 Shamai St. (☎ 02/623-7000; www.bimot.co.il).

No phone. Performances can vary from free to hundreds of shekels. Inquire at ticket agencies (see Ticket Agencies, above).

★ **Targ Music Center** EIN KAREM The Targ Music Center, aka The Ein Karem Music Center or the Eden-Tamir Music Center, hosts weekly recitals and classical music concerts on alternate Friday afternoons and Saturday evenings. *29 HaMa'ayan St. ☎ 02/641-4250. www.einkeremusi center.org.il. Tickets NIS 50–NIS 70.*

★ **The Train Puppet Theatre** LIBERTY BELL PARK   A favorite for families with children, this theater has developed an international reputation for its performances featuring puppets and marionettes. *See p 54,* ⑫.

Orchestras & Repertories

The Israel Camerata, Jerusalem   This highly acclaimed chamber music orchestra performs throughout the country and the world; it also attracts internationally renowned soloists and choirs for its performances in Jerusalem. The programming can also be innovative: One season incorporated puppetry from Spain. The orchestra performs primarily in the Jerusalem Theatre, but also occasionally at the YMCA. *206 Jaffa Rd. (administrative offices). ☎ 02/502-0503. www.jcamerata. com/en. Tickets NIS 100–NIS 150.*

JEST   Jerusalem English-Speaking Theatre is a company of amateur actors that performs several plays a year, at different venues around town. *☎ 02/642-0908. www.jest-theatre.org. Tickets NIS 30–NIS 60.*

The Jerusalem Symphony Orchestra   The JSO is the official orchestra of the Israel Broadcasting Authority and the resident orchestra of the Jerusalem Theatre. It has been in existence since before the establishment of the State of Israel. *Henry Crown Hall, 5 Chopin St. ☎ 02/561-1498. www.jso.co.il. Tickets NIS 90-NIS170.*

Galleries & Permanent Exhibitions

★★★ **Holocaust Art Museum** YAD VASHEM   Not surprisingly, Yad Vashem's collection of Holocaust art is the largest in the world, comprising some 10,000 works created during the Shoah (Holocaust). The collection of drawings—many on irregular scraps of paper, and using paints or ink improvised from whatever material was on hand—is extraordinarily moving, providing a glimpse into the overwhelming innate desire of humankind to overcome and express emotions creatively, even under the most horrifying of circumstances. *Mt. of Remembrance. ☎ 02/644-3600. www.yadvashem.org. Free admission. Sun–Wed 9am–5pm, Thurs 9am–8pm, Fri 9am–2pm.*

The Holocaust Art Museum is home to more than 10,000 works.

★★ Jerusalem Artists House (Beit HaOmanim) DOWNTOWN

In this historic building (see p 46, ❹), the Jerusalem headquarters of the Israel Association of Painters and Sculptors showcases local, national, and international artists in a changing array of one-person and group exhibits. The organization also uses art to build bridges for peace, spearheading projects designed to foster mutual tolerance and understanding among Israeli and Palestinian schoolchildren. The Artists House staff can put you in touch with any artist whose work interests you and arrange the shipping of your purchase. *12 Shmuel Ha-Nagid St. ☎ 02/ 625-2636. www.art.org.il. Free admission. Gallery Sun–Thurs 10am–1pm & 4–7pm, Fri 10am–1pm.*

★★ kids L.A. Mayer Memorial Museum for Islamic Art KIRYAT SHMUEL

This museum houses hundreds of objets d'art collected from the Muslim world, including ceramic ware, textiles, figurines, tiles, glass, metalwork, and jewelry. There are also stunning examples of illuminated calligraphy—and, as part of a separate collection, an amazing assortment of antique clocks and watches (many from 18th-century Europe), as well as unique examples of music boxes, automaton machinery, and the early technology of meteorological equipment. *2 HaPalmach St. ☎ 02/566-1291. www.islamicart.co.il/en. Admission NIS 40 adults, NIS 30 students, NIS 20 children & seniors. Sun, Mon, Wed & Thurs 10am–3pm; Tues 10am–6pm; Fri & Sat 10am–2pm.*

★★★ Museum on the Seam

RTE. 1   Hailed by the *New York Times* as one of 29 art venues in the world that "open your eyes and blow your mind," this thought-provoking museum focuses on the thorny issues of social justice, stereotypes, and Arab-Jewish coexistence (the "seam" refers to the unofficial border between East and West Jerusalem, on which the museum lies). It is advisable to call first and inquire about guided tours (no extra charge) in order to get the most out of the unusual exhibits. *4 Hel Handasa St. ☎ 02/638-1278. www.mots.org.il. Admission NIS 25 adults, NIS 10 students & seniors. Sun, Mon, Wed & Thurs 10am–5pm; Tues 10am–9pm; Fri 10am–2pm.*

★ Sir Isaac and Lady Edith Wolfson Museum REHAVIA

The headquarters of Israel's Chief Rabbinate is the home of one of the city's lesser-known treasures: the Wolfson family's private collection of Judaica, comprising antique Chanukah menorahs, *kiddush* cups (ceremonial wine goblets), wedding contracts, *mezuzot* (sacred parchment holders affixed to the doors of Jewish households), adornments to Torah scrolls, and more. Although only a fraction of the precious objects in the collection are exhibited at any one time, these unique items gathered from the four corners of the Jewish diaspora are worth walking the few blocks from downtown Jerusalem to view. *In Heichal Shlomo, 56 King George St.* ☎ *02/624-7112. Admission NIS 25 Sun–Thur 9am–3pm..*

★ The U. Nahon Museum of Italian Jewish Art DOWNTOWN

In addition to the life-size replica of the northern Italian synagogue (see p 47, ⑨), there is a small collection of art, clothing, and furniture from Italy, but disappointingly little Judaica. There are beautiful photographs on the ground floor, before reaching the ticket counter. *27 Hillel St.* ☎ *02/624-1610. www.jija.org. Admission NIS 15 adults, NIS 10 students, NIS 7.50 seniors. Sun, Tues & Wed 9am–5pm; Mon 9am–2pm; Thurs & Fri 9am–1pm.*

Film

★★ The Jerusalem Cinematheque HEBRON RD.

This modern building in the valley between East and West Jerusalem contains a cinematic museum, as well as comfortable screening rooms for films from all over the world. It also plays host to the annual Jerusalem Film Festival, held every summer. *11 Hebron Rd.* ☎ *02/565-4333. www.jer-cin.org.il. Tickets NIS 36.*

★★ The Jerusalem Theater TALBIEH

Daily evening (and occasional matinee) screenings of first-run films, as well as classics. *20 Marcus St., corner of Chopin St.* ☎ *02/560-5757. www.jerusalem-theatre.co.il. Tickets NIS 35.*

★ Semadar Theater GERMAN COLONY

The city's last remaining full-screen movie theater has new, comfortable seats and shows first releases. The on-site cafe serves beer to moviegoers and restaurant customers. *4 George Lloyd St.* ☎ *02/566-0954. Tickets NIS 35.*

Bars, Pubs, Cafes & Clubs

Avram Bar Café DOWNTOWN

Perhaps the most ambitious venue in the city, Avram's has live music every day of the week except Sundays. Open during the day as a cafe-restaurant, musical performances begin at 9:30pm (1pm on Fri). *97 Jaffa Rd. (corner of Kiach St., Davidka Sq.).* ☎ *077/445-0701. Tickets NIS 25–NIS 35.*

Bolinat DOWNTOWN

A hip place for dancing at night and drinking smooth alcoholic shakes any time of day. The party starts early on Fridays. *6 Dorot Rishonim St.* ☎ *02/624-9733. No cover charge. Open 24 hr.*

Borderline EAST JERUSALEM

One of the best bars in the eastern side of the city, where knowledgeable waiters dispense an assortment of sweet tobaccos for smoking in

Museum on the Seam has been lauded by the New York Times.

nargila (hookah) water pipes. *13 Shimon Hatzadik St.* ☎ *02/532-8432. www.shahwan.org.*

★★ **Bulghourji Lounge and Gardens** OLD CITY One of the few Armenian restaurants in town, the outdoor patio is the loveliest place to have a drink in East Jerusalem, if not the entire city. *6 Armenian Patriarchate Rd.* ☎ *02/628-2080.*

★★ **Mia Bar** DOWNTOWN Quite possibly the best stocked bar in Jerusalem, Mia also gives courses in beer, wine, and whiskey appreciation. Its bartenders are among the most professional in the city. *18 Hillel St.* ☎ *02/625-9491. www.mia-bar.co.il.*

★★ **Mirror Bar** MAMILLA The décor here is no surprise: mirrors line the walls and reflect the glitz and glitter of the upscale crowd that gathers here every night of the week. If you're coming to mix and mingle, don't bother to show up before 10pm. *11 Shlomo Hamelekh St., in the Mamilla Hotel.* ☎ *02/548-2230. www.mamillahotel.com. AE, DC, MC, V.*

Stardust NAHALAT SHIVA An eclectic place, Stardust doubles as a sports bar, televising major football (soccer) matches and basketball games on a big-screen TV. Its extended happy hour features rum-and-cokes for NIS 10, bottles of wine for NIS 40, and similar bargains. In the summer months, reggae parties welcome in the weekend on Friday afternoons. *6 Rivlin St.* ☎ *02/622-2196. www.pubstardust.com.*

Yellow Submarine TALPIOT This not-for-profit club showcases up-and-coming musicians representing all genres. It has recently instituted jazz nights every Tuesday at 9:30pm. *13 HaRekhavim St.* ☎ *02/679-4040. www.yellowsubmarine.org.il.*

Zolli's/Nadin NAHALAT SHIVA This pair of adjoining nightspots are under the same ownership and run mostly identical specials. The gimmicks behind their success: complimentary *nargilas,* and every beer comes with a free shot—provided you show student ID (as you can imagine, it draws a youngish crowd). You'll recognize Zolli's by the outdoor tables with baskets of free popcorn. *5 Rivlin St.* ☎ *054/812-4200.* ●

Yellow Submarine has jazz nights every Tuesday.

West Jerusalem Lodging

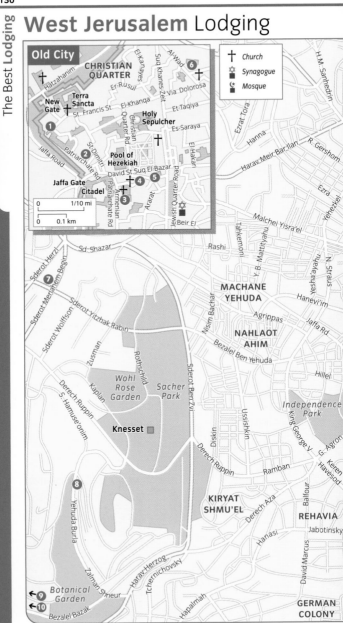

Old City

† Church
☆ Synagogue
☪ Mosque

CHRISTIAN QUARTER

Hatzanahim

El-Ka'Ayes

Suq Khanes-Zeit

Al-Wad

Via Dolorosa

6

Er-Rusul

New Gate

Terra Sancta

St. Francis St.

El-Khanqa

Quarter Rd

Christian Quarter Rd

Et-Taqiya

Holy Sepulcher

Es-Saraya

1

St-Dimitri

Patriarchate Rd

Pool of Hezekiah

El-Hakari

Jaffa Road

2

David St · Suq El-Bazar

4 **5**

Jaffa Gate

Citadel

3

Armenian

Ararat

Patriarchate Rd

Jewish Quarter Road

☆

Beir El

☪

0 — 1/10 mi

0 — 0.1 km

H.M. Sanhedrin

Ezrat Tora

Hanna

Harav Meir Bar-Ilan

R. Gershom

Ezra

Yehezkel

Sd. Shazar

Malchei Yisra'el

N. Straus

Rashi

Tahkemoni

Y. B. Mattityahu

Yesha'ayahu

MACHANE YEHUDA

Nisim Bachar

Hanevi'im

Sderot Herzl

7

Sderot Menahem Begin

Sderot Wolffson

Sderot Yitzhak Rabin

Zusman

Agrippas

NAHLAOT AHIM

Bezalel Ben Yehuda

Jaffa Rd

Hillel

Kaplan

Rothschild

Wohl Rose Garden

Sacher Park

Sderot Ben Zvi

Independence Park

King George V.

G. Agron

Keren Hayesod

S. Hamuse'onim

Derech Ruppin

Knesset ■

Diskin

Derech Ruppin

Ussishkin

Ramban

Balfour

REHAVIA

8

Yehuda Burla

KIRYAT SHMU'EL

Derech Aza

Hanasi

Jabotinsky

David Marcus

← **9**

← **10**

Botanical Garden

Zalman Shneur

Harav Herzog

Tchernichovsky

Hapalmah

Bezalel Bazak

GERMAN COLONY

Previous page: The Inbal Hotel is a popular conference venue.

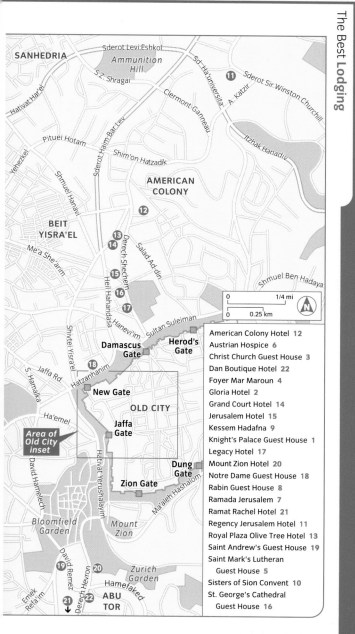

American Colony Hotel 12
Austrian Hospice 6
Christ Church Guest House 3
Dan Boutique Hotel 22
Foyer Mar Maroun 4
Gloria Hotel 2
Grand Court Hotel 14
Jerusalem Hotel 15
Kessem Hadafna 9
Knight's Palace Guest House 1
Legacy Hotel 17
Mount Zion Hotel 20
Notre Dame Guest House 18
Rabin Guest House 8
Ramada Jerusalem 7
Ramat Rachel Hotel 21
Regency Jerusalem Hotel 11
Royal Plaza Olive Tree Hotel 13
Saint Andrew's Guest House 19
Saint Mark's Lutheran
  Guest House 5
Sisters of Sion Convent 10
St. George's Cathedral
  Guest House 16

East Jerusalem Lodging

0   1/4 mi
0   0.25 km

A. Wallenberg
Ezrat
Straus St.
Harav Agan
Agrippas
Shomron
Mesilat Yesharim
Eliash
Jaffa Rd
Yabez
Harav Kook
Hahavatzelet
Monbaz
Heleni Hamalka
Hyrcanus
Ben Hillel
Luncz
Salomon
Hahistadrut
Ben-Yehuda St.
Shamai
Bianchini
Rivlin St.
Ha Soreg
S. Ben Shetah
Jerusalem
Courtyard
Be'en
Shmuel Hanagid
Hillel
Shlomtzion Hamalka
Uzi Hasson
Coresh
Jaffa Rd
Shacham
Yanai
Shlomo Hamelech
MAMILLA
Sherman
Garden
Rabbi Akiva
King George V
Avida
Gan
Ha'atzma'ut
(Independence Park)
Menashe Ben Yisra'el
Ha'emek
REHAVIA
K.K. Levisra'el
Alharizi
Ibn Gabirol
Ibn Ezra
Gershon Agron
Zamenhof
Hess
Shema
Ramban
Lincoln
Paul Emil Botta
Maimon
Arlosoroff
Balfour
Smolenskin
Keren Hayesod
Washington
King David St.
Mapu
Bloomfield
Garden
Derech Aza
Ovadia Mibertinoro
Brenner
Ahad Ha'am
Sokolow
Kikar
Chile
M.M. Sfarim
S. Aleichem
Molcho
Ze'ev Jabotinsky

Agron Guest House 10	Jerusalem Gold 1	Mamilla Hotel 6
Beit Shmuel Guest House 12	Jerusalem Inn Hotel 3	Montefiore Hotel 5
Dan Panorama Jerusalem 16	King David Hotel 15	Rosary Convent
David Citadel 7	Leonardo Plaza 9	Guest House 11
Eldan Hotel 13	Lev Yerushalayim	Three Arches Hotel –
Harmony Hotel 4	Suite Hotel 2	YMCA 14
Inbal Hotel 17	Little House in Rechavia 8	

Lodging Best Bets

Best Breakfast Buffet
★★★ David Citadel Hotel $$$$
7 King David St. (p 135)

Best Views
★★ St. Andrew's Scottish Guest
House $$ *1 David Remez St. (p 140)*

Best For Kids
★ Ramat Rachel Hotel $$ *Kibbutz
Ramat Rachel (p 139)*

Best Prestigious Hotel
★★★ King David Hotel $$$$
23 King David St. (p 137)

Best Old City Guest House
★★ Knight's Palace $ *Freres St.
(p 137)*

Best Location
★★ Harmony Hotel $$ *6 Yoel
Salomon St. (p 136)*

Best Spa & Pool
★★★ Regency Hotel $$$ *32 Lehi
St. (p 139)*

Best Hotel for Romance
★★★ Mount Zion Hotel $$$$
17 Hebron Rd. (p 138)

Best New Hotel
★★★ Mamilla Hotel $$$$
11 Shlomo Hamelekh St. (p 138)

Best Terrace
★★ Dan Boutique $$ *31 Hebron
Rd. (p 135)*

Best Hotel for Business
★★★ Inbal $$$ *3 Jabotinsky St.
(p 136)*

Best Cosmopolitan Clientele
★★★ American Colony Hotel $$$
2 Louis Vincent St. (p 134)

Knight's Palace is an excellent guest house in the Old City.

Jerusalem Lodging A to Z

Travel tip

You can often score a significant discount for one night if you agree to check in after sunset on a Saturday, since hotels allow their Sabbath-observing Jewish guests to stay in their rooms until then; if you are already a guest, you may request late check-out (at no extra charge) for the same reason.

★ **Agron Guest House** FRANCE SQUARE   Centrally located in West Jerusalem, this upgraded hostel represents good value when it is not booked by teenage tour groups, which is usually the case in summers. TV and Wi-Fi add to the appeal. *6 Agron St.* ☎ *02/594-5522. www.iyha.org.il/eng. 55 units. Doubles NIS 340–NIS 400; bed in dorm room NIS 114. AE, DC, MC, V. Map p 132.*

★★★ **American Colony Hotel** EAST JERUSALEM   The American Colony is to East Jerusalem what the King David is to West Jerusalem: understated elegance and the hotel of choice for the entertainment and political elite. The preferred meeting place for Palestinian and Israeli business and journalistic contacts. *2 Louis Vincent St. (corner of Nablus Rd.).* ☎ *02/627-9777. www. americancolony.com. 92 units. Doubles $275–$850. AE, DC, MC, V. Map p 130.*

★ **Austrian Hospice** OLD CITY   This large 19th-century building is one of the closest guest houses to the Temple Mount; the view from the rooftop is indescribable. Large rooms (some triples), a great coffee shop, and garden. *37 Via Dolorosa.* ☎ *02/626-5800. www. austrianhospice.com. 34 units, plus dormitory facilities. Doubles $130 (prices will be quoted in Euros). Map p 130.*

★ **Beit Shmuel Guest House** MAMILLA   Part of a large complex designed by Moshe Safdie (1938–) for the World Union for Progressive (Reform) Judaism. There are rooms for couples or families, a newer Shimshon Center with upgraded rooms, and even one studio apartment. *13 King David St. (entrance around the corner at 3 Shamia St.).* ☎ *02/620-3455. www.beitshmuel.com/english. 50 units. Shimshon Center doubles*

The American Colony Hotel is a favorite meeting place for both Palestinians and Israelis.

A room in the Dan Panorama Jerusalem.

$149–$179, Beit Shmuel doubles $99–$119. AE, MC, V. Map p 132.

★ Christ Church Guest House

OLD CITY   The guest house is in a surprisingly large and peaceful compound for its great location, right opposite the Tower of David and just inside Jaffa Gate. There are pleasant open places to relax outside your simple room, amidst the conviviality of an international clientele. *Armenian Patriarchate Rd. ☎ 02/627-7727. www.cmj-israel.org. Doubles $100. MC, V. Map p 130.*

★★ Dan Boutique Hotel

HEBRON RD.   A truly fine moderately priced hotel across from the old railway yard that is becoming a new hub for entertainment and restaurants. *31 Hebron Rd. ☎ 02/568-9999. www.danhotels.com. 126 units. Doubles $158–$220. AE, DC, MC, V. Map p 130.*

★★ Dan Panorama Jerusalem

TALBIEH   Part of the well-regarded Dan chain that owns the King David Hotel, the Dan Panorama is just a notch lower than its fancier sister around the corner. It has a recently renovated lobby, and the rooms are constantly being upgraded. *39 Keren Hayesod St. ☎ 02/569-5695. www.danhotels.com. 292 units. Doubles $230–$320. AE, DC, MC, V. Map p 132.*

★★★ David Citadel

KING DAVID ST.   This luxury property is becoming a hotel of choice for visiting dignitaries, rivaling the stately King David. Every room has a magnificent view of the Old City. *7 King David St. ☎ 02/621-1111. www.thedavidcitadel.com. 384 units. Doubles $440–$630. AE, DC, MC, V. Map p 132.*

★ Eldan Hotel

KING DAVID ST.   A moderately priced hotel owned and managed by Eldan, Israel's largest car-rental company. Well maintained, but the only hotel on this street with no pool. *24 King David*

Dollars vs. Shekels

Unlike prices for everything else in Israel, prices for hotel rooms, international flights, and car rentals are usually quoted in U.S. dollars (USD). Tourists paying for these items in foreign currency (such as using a credit card) are exempt from the country's 16.5% Value Added Tax (VAT). If you eat lunch or dinner at your hotel and charge the meal to your room, you also don't have to pay the VAT.

Every room at the David Citadel has a magnificent view of the Old City.

St. ☎ 02/567-9777. www.eldan hotel.com. 76 units. Doubles $190–$240. AE, DC, MC, V. Map p 132.

Foyer Mar Maroun OLD CITY Not far from Jaffa Gate, the Maronite Patriarchate's guest house is hidden away on a quiet, winding lane. The highlight is the roof, where thoughtfully placed benches allow you to enjoy the fabulous view of the Dome of the Rock in relative comfort. *25 Maronite Convent St. ☎ 02/628-2158. www.maronite jerusalem.org. 27 units. Doubles $90. No credit cards. Map p 130.*

★ **Gloria Hotel** OLD CITY Self-styled as a hotel rather than a guest house, the Gloria is one of the better choices in the Old City. Check out the rooms in both the main building and the annex across the street. *33 Latin Patriarchate Rd. ☎ 02/628-2431. www.gloria-hotel. com. 94 units. Doubles $120–$140. AE, V. Map p 130.*

★★ **Grand Court Hotel** RTE. 1 Located on the dividing line between East and West Jerusalem, this is one of the city's largest hotels. Rooms are comfortable, and there is a commendable (kosher) breakfast buffet. *15 St. George St. ☎ 02/591-7777. www. grandcourt.co.il. 442 units. Doubles $180–$280. AE, DC, MC, V. Map p 130.*

★★ **Harmony Hotel** NAHALAT SHIVA A new moderately priced hotel (it opened in 2008), the six-story Harmony has a terrific location in the pedestrian restaurant district. There is

a daily complimentary happy hour, with wine and canapés. *6 Yoel Salomon St. ☎ 02/621-9999. www.atlas. co.il. 50 units. Doubles $200–$275. AE, DC, MC, V. Map p 132.*

★★★ **kids Inbal Hotel** LIBERTY BELL PARK A classy hotel that is favored by upscale professional groups for prestigious conferences. There is swimming all year-round, and Liberty Bell Park for the kids is right next door. *3 Jabotinsky St. ☎ 02/675-6666. www.inbalhotel. com. 287 units. Doubles $300–$575. AE, DC, MC, V. Map p 132.*

★★ **Jerusalem Gold** CENTRAL BUS STATION Conveniently located for catching both urban and intercity buses, this hotel is also a good choice for those requiring handicapped access; it even has Braille markings for all rooms. *234 Jaffa Rd. ☎ 02/501-3333. www.jerusalemgold.com. 196 units. Doubles $260–$390. AE, DC, MC, V. Map p 132.*

★★ **Jerusalem Hotel** EAST JERUSALEM The Arab sector's finest boutique-style hotel, run by a family with generations of experience in the hospitality industry. *Nablus Rd. (entrance at 4 Antara Ben-Shadad St.). ☎ 800/657-9401 or 02/628-3282. www.jrshotel.com. 15 units. Doubles $190–$240. AE, DC, MC, V. Map p 130.*

★ **Jerusalem Inn Hotel** DOWNTOWN Arguably the best budget hotel in the city; no lobby or elevator, but a good location and better

Israeli Breakfast Buffets

Among American travelers in particular, the breakfast buffets offered by Israeli hotels have evoked wonder for their bounty and variety. Israelis disdain meat for breakfast in favor of more wholesome food such as cheese, fish, and salad. Moreover, virtually all West Jerusalem hotels maintain kosher dining rooms (see p 117). Travelers on a budget often make sandwiches for lunch from the munificent breakfast. Unless otherwise indicated in this chapter, breakfast is included in your payment for the room.

rooms than most places in this price category. *7 Hyrcanos St.* ☎ *02/625-2757. www.jerusalem-inn.com. 23 units. Doubles $120–$170. MC, V. Map p 132.*

★★ Kessem Hadafna EIN
KAREM · While the rooms here are in a modern structure, the views from the spacious individual porches give this place its quaint charm. There are two charming rooms for couples and an apartment with kitchenette for families. Because of the multitude of cafes in town, no breakfast is served. *15 Hadafna St.* ☎ *050/427-4416. 3 units. Doubles NIS 500 weekdays; NIS 650 weekends, 2-night min. MC, V. Map p 130.*

★★★ King David Hotel KING
DAVID ST. When you stay here, you stake your claim to a little piece

of history, as the hotel has welcomed a who's-who of dignitaries. Impeccable service from a staff used to dealing with royalty and celebrity. *23 King David St.* ☎ *02/620-8888. www.danhotels.com. 237 units. Doubles $490–$690. AE, DC, MC, V. Map p 132.*

★★ Knight's Palace Guest
House OLD CITY A real gem located between Jaffa Gate and New Gate, this guest house is part of the headquarters of the Latin Patriarchate. Unusual for the Old City, the rooms have air-conditioning, direct-dial telephones, and even televisions with satellite reception. *Freres St. (corner of Latin Patriarchate Rd.).* ☎ *02/628-2537. www.knights palace.com. 50 units. Doubles $140–$160. MC, V. Map p 130.*

The King David Hotel frequently caters to royalty and celebrities.

★★ **Legacy Hotel** EAST JERUSA-LEM   After undergoing a total reno-vation in 2008, this property has now transcended its YMCA image and is solidly in the category of a good tourist hotel. *29 Nablus Rd.* ☎ *02/627-0800. www.jerusalem legacy.com. 49 units. Doubles $150–$170. AE, DC, MC, V. Map p 130.*

★★★ **Leonardo Plaza** INDEPEN-DENCE PARK   Until recently part of the Sheraton chain (where it went by the name Jerusalem Plaza), the Plaza is conveniently located a short walk from the Ben Yehuda Street pedestrian mall and right on the fringe of Independence Park. As is custom-ary in Jerusalem, the rooms with ter-rific views of the Old City cost more. *47 King George St.* ☎ *800/325-3535 or 02/629-8666. www.moriahhotels. com. 300 units. Doubles $350–$400. AE, DC, MC, V. Map p 132.*

★★ kids **Lev Yerushalayim Suite Hotel** DOWNTOWN Unbeatable location as the hotel closest to the Ben Yehuda Street pedestrian mall. Suites with kitchen-ettes and convertible living room sofas make it a good choice for fam-ilies. *18 King George St.* ☎ *02/530-0333. www.levyerushalayim.co.il. 97 units. Doubles $185–$205. AE, DC, MC, V. Map p 132.*

★★ **Little House in Rechavia** REHAVIA   Tucked away in this quiet, prestigious neighborhood close to downtown is a small hotel with homey and comfortable rooms. Adding to the serenity are the shaded patios where you can sip unlimited free tea or coffee. Its sis-ter hotels are equally charming: **Little House in Bakah** and **Little House in the Moshava (Colony).** *20 Eben Ezra St.* ☎ *02/563-3344. www.jerusalem-hotel.co.il. 28 units. Doubles $129–$189. AE, DC, MC, V. Map p 132.*

★★★ **Mamilla Hotel** MAMILLA The most stylish boutique hotel in Jerusalem, open only since June 2009, is under the same ownership as the David Citadel. It is conve-niently attached to the new Alrov Mamilla shopping promenade. *11 Shlomo Hamelekh St.* ☎ *02/548-2230. www.mamillahotel.com. 194 units. Doubles $350–$650. AE, DC, MC, V. Map p 132.*

★★ **Montefiore Hotel** DOWN-TOWN   In a terrific location and under excellent management, this six-story hotel represents good value. It underwent a complete refurbishment in the fall of 2009. *7 Schatz St.* ☎ *02/622-1111. www. montefiorehotel.com. 48 units. Doubles $159–$199. AE, DC, MC, V. Map p 132.*

★★★ kids **Mount Zion Hotel** HEBRON RD.   From the architec-ture and interior design to the mag-nificent views and the friendly, efficient staff, a stay here just might be the most satisfying overall hotel

The Mount Zion Hotel offers magnificent views.

The Notre Dame Guest House is located in one of the city's most spectacular buildings.

experience in the city. A massage in the *hammam* (Turkish bath) is a unique experience, and it is tempting to stay in the Jacuzzi too long. *17 Hebron Rd.* ☎ *02/568-9555. www. mountzion.co.il. 137 units. $280–$400. AE, DC, MC, V. Map p 130.*

★★ Notre Dame Guest House

NEW GATE   Located in one of Jerusalem's most spectacular buildings, the New Gate to the Old City is right across the street; it is also within easy walking distance of downtown West Jerusalem. A favorite with Roman Catholic pilgrimage groups. *3 Hativat Hatzanhanim (just off Tzahal Sq.).* ☎ *02/627-9111. www.notredame center.org. 145 units. Doubles $150–$184. MC, V. Map p 130.*

★ Rabin Guest House NEVE

SHA'ANAN   The newest and most modern YHA-affiliated guest house in Jerusalem, the rooms are spacious and well equipped for this price range. *1 Nahman Avigad St.* ☎ *02/678-0101. www.iyha.org.il/ eng. 77 units. Doubles NIS 410; bed in dorm room NIS 140. AE, DC, MC, V. Map p 130.*

★★★ Ramada Jerusalem HERZL

BLVD.   The former Renaissance is now an upgraded Ramada-Wyndham property. Good choice of standard, connecting, and executive rooms. Discounts for stays of 7 days and/or opting out of breakfast. Free downtown shuttle service. *Glatt kosher. Herzl Blvd at Ruppin Bridge.* ☎ *02/659-9999. www.ramada.com. 306 units. Doubles $160–$390. AE, DC, MC, V. Map p 130.*

★ kids Ramat Rachel Hotel KIB-

BUTZ RAMAT RACHEL   Poor service is the major shortcoming of this establishment, but families might consider it for the outdoor facilities: a huge swimming pool, night-lit tennis and basketball courts, and a playground for the younger ones. Great views of Bethlehem and the Judean desert. *Kibbutz Ramat Rachel.* ☎ *888/669-5700 or 02/670-2555. www.ramatrachel.co.il. 164 units. Doubles $176–$230. AE, DC, MC, V. Map p 130.*

★★★ Regency Jerusalem

Hotel MT. SCOPUS   This stunningly designed hotel is popular with locals for its fitness center, tennis courts, and two swimming pools (indoor and outdoor). It also boasts extra perks such as: executive floors with a VIP lounge; a discount for opting out of breakfast; and a free shuttle service into the city. *32 Lehi St.* ☎ *02/533-1234. www.regency. co.il. 503 units. Doubles $150–$180. AE, DC, MC, V. Map p 130.*

The Regency Jerusalem Hotel boasts lots of extra perks and amenities.

Rosary Convent Guest House and Hostel INDEPENDENCE PARK An Old City–style Christian guest house with lovely grounds just across Independence Park from downtown. Good value for solo travelers, as they pay half the price of a double. *14 Agron St.* ☎ *02/625-8529. 23 units. Doubles $120. No credit cards. Map p 132.*

★★ **Royal Plaza Olive Tree Hotel** RTE. 1 Located in the same hotel row as the Grand Court and the Moriah Classic, this hotel has the nicest interior design of the three. It is popular with group tours. *23 St. George St.* ☎ *02/541-0410. www.olivetreehotel.com. 304 units. Doubles $260–$330. AE, DC, MC, V. Map p 130.*

★★ **Saint Andrew's Guest House** OLD RAILWAY STATION A cut above the typical Christian guest house, this Church of Scotland property is more like a boutique hotel. With its great views and friendly staff, this is one of the rare Jerusalem properties that is heavily booked all year round. *1 David Remez St.* ☎ *02/673-2401. www.scotsguesthouse.com. 20 units. Doubles $125–$160. MC, V. Map p 130.*

Saint Andrew's Guest House is popular year-round.

★ **Saint Mark's Lutheran Guest House** OLD CITY The atmospheric rooms here are of Jerusalem stone; most bathrooms have showers only. The site is shared by, but separated from, the Evangelical Lutheran Hostel. Free coffee and tea are served. Call for directions before arrival and arrange a baggage porter to meet you. *Saint Mark's Rd.* ☎ *02/626-8888. www.luth-guest house-jerusalem.com. 23 units. Doubles $120 (prices denominated in Euros). No credit cards. Map p 130.*

Sisters of Sion Convent EIN KAREM Just what you'd expect from a guest house on convent grounds: basic rooms, sparsely furnished; small en suite bathrooms; everything spotlessly clean. Rated above its counterparts in the Old City for the tranquility of its beautiful gardens, but it is a bit far from most sightseeing. *Ha-Oren St.* ☎ *02/641-5738. 34 units. Doubles $120. No credit cards. Map p 130.*

★ **St. George's Cathedral Guest House** EAST JERUSALEM A very attractive place to stay, with the rooms cloistered around an English garden hidden from the street by high walls. Rooms vary, so pick one you like. The staff is knowledgeable and helpful. *20 Nablus Rd.* ☎ *02/628-3302. 24 units. Doubles $100–$120. MC, V. Map p 130.*

★ **Three Arches Hotel** KING DAVID ST. This is the YMCA building (see p 65, ❶), but it is not your typical hostel-like YMCA hotel. More than a few rooms could stand some touching up. Great terrace for al fresco dining. *26 King David St.* ☎ *02/569-2692. www.ymca3arch.co.il. 56 units. Doubles $143–$190. AE, DC, MC, V. Map p 132.* ●

The Dead Sea & Masada

1. Masada
2. Dead Sea Beach
3. Ein Gedi National Park
4. Ahava Visitors' Center
5. Enot Tsukim Nature Reserve
6. Qumran
7. Inn of the Good Samaritan

Previous page: Old Jaffa in Tel Aviv dates back thousands of years.

Just 30 minutes by car from Jerusalem is one the great natural wonders of the world. History has also been made here: The ruins of the wall of Jericho are thought to be mankind's oldest fortifications, dating back an astounding 9,000 years; Qumran is where the Dead Sea scrolls were discovered and John the Baptist might have lived. Finally, there is Masada—after Jerusalem, the most emotionally laden site in all of Israel. It is possible to see both Qumran and Masada, and have a dip in the Dead Sea, in one day; in order to have a relaxing trip, however—including enjoying Mother Nature's gifts of Dead Sea mud and/or the oasis of Ein Gedi—I recommend an overnight stay. START: **Route 1 to Jerusalem Dead Sea Hwy via Mount Scopus.**

West Bank travel

Travel restrictions in the West Bank can change suddenly, so always check current conditions before traveling through this region. While cars rented in Israel are not insured for travel in the West Bank and Gaza, most companies do permit travel on Hwy. 1, the main east-west highway from Jerusalem to The Dead Sea, and Route 90. Clarify these regulations each time you rent a car and get explicit instructions as to how to get to these roads in the West Bank, making sure not to stray anywhere else in the West Bank with your rental car. Similar conditions may apply to your medical insurance policy, so check with your provider before entering the region.

❶ ★★★ **Masada.** Now a UNESCO World Heritage Site, Masada is both a magnificent remnant of Herodian engineering and construction, and a symbol of Jewish heroism: the site of the rebels' last stand against the Romans and their choice of mass suicide over being taken captive (two women hid in a well and survived to tell the story). The stirring

Masada is a UNESCO World Heritage Site.

"Swimming" in the Dead Sea

The sea is called "dead" because it is so salty—the most mineral-laden waters in the world—that no life can survive in its waters. If you have cuts or scrapes on your skin, you will most certainly feel them; you'll also want to not let the water get into your eyes. Do not plunge in; gently lie back from a quasi-sitting position: The buoyancy is the whole point of the experience. Most of your body will stay above the surface of the water. For a fun photo-op, bring a newspaper to read in your liquid "easy chair."

While the Dead Sea will still be here in our lifetimes, it is, most unfortunately, shrinking at an alarming rate. One side effect is the spontaneous appearance of sinkholes along the Dead Sea shoreline. Dangerous areas have been fenced off and posted with warning signs: Obey them!

credo "Masada shall not fall again" is what motivates the citizen-soldiers of Israel (who take their oaths of allegiance on this cliff-top) to defend their beleaguered country against its neighboring enemies. There are 45 steep steps to climb after the cable car ride to the site. Masada may also be climbed by the hardy: There is no charge to be led by a park ranger up the Snake Path, a 50-minute climb up a winding gravel path that starts at 4:45am & arrives in time to watch the sun rise over the Dead Sea. ⏱ 2–3 hr.

Dead Sea Beach is 416m (1,365 feet) below sea level.

Masada National Park. ☎ 08/658-4207. Admission (entrance to site & Yigal Yadin Masada Museum, a pamphlet with map of the site & cable car ride) NIS 49 adults, NIS 26 children; admission to site only NIS 25 adults, NIS 13 children; portable audio guides can be rented for NIS 24. Cable cars operate Sun–Thurs Oct–Mar 8am–4pm, Apr–Sept 8am–5pm; Fri year-round 8am–2pm.

② ★★ **Dead Sea Beach.** There are a number of beaches along the Dead Sea where one can enter the water, but I recommend the one at the **Ein Gedi Sulphur Springs and Spa**—one major reason being that The Lowest Spot on Earth (–416m/–1,365 ft.) is here. The facilities include a swimming pool, beach chairs, troughs of Dead Sea mud, pools of healthful mineral-rich water, indoor and outdoor showers, and locker rooms and towels. There is a restaurant-snack bar here, but its high prices make it worth your while to pack a picnic. ⏱ 1½ hr. Rte. 90. ☎ 08/659-4221. www.ein-gedi.co.il. Admission NIS 65 adults Sun–Fri; NIS 70 adults Sat & Jewish holidays. Daily 8am–6pm (until 5pm in winter).

A mountain goat at Ein Gedi National Park.

❸ Ein Gedi National Park. This popular park comprises two very different sections: the **Antiquities Park** and the **Nature Reserve.** It is here that a unique mosaic floor of a 6th-century synagogue has been uncovered, depicting a circle design of peacock chicks and adult birds. In another part of the park are the ruins of a Chalcolithic (Copper Age) sanctuary that dates back some 5,000 years. The nature reserve's spectacular waterfalls and hiking trails are within the **Nahal David** and **Nahal Arugot** canyons. Fortunately, the best falls are also the easiest to get to: An upward walk of 15 to 20 minutes through palm trees and under canopies of papyrus reeds leads to the Nahal David Falls, where it is great fun to stand and luxuriate under the cooling water; be sure to wear a bathing suit under your hiking clothes. Maps and suggested trail routes are included in the admission fee.

Getting There

Although frequent Egged buses ply the route from Jerusalem to all points on the Dead Sea (www.egged.co.il/eng), it is advisable either to take an organized tour or rent a car. Bus tours leave virtually daily, picking passengers up from hotels; check your hotel lobby for leaflets. Hertz is the only car rental company with offices in both the capital and Ein Bokek, the Dead Sea's commercial center, and their prices are competitive (☎ 02/623-1351; www.hertz.co.il/en). If you are considering touring Jericho, verify whether your car insurance is valid there; in all other areas in the region, there is no problem (it is best to tour Jericho with a guide anyway; this can be arranged beforehand in Jerusalem). Be sure to keep plenty of drinking water in the car at all times; the weather can cause dehydration all year round.

Staying Overnight

Most of the region's hotels are clustered in Ein Bokek, at the southern end of the Dead Sea. However, I cannot recommend staying there: These impersonal hotels are geared towards groups (or patients who are there for medical treatments, especially for psoriasis) and do not trouble themselves to give decent service to individual travelers. On the other hand, there are guest houses and vacation cottages that offer perfectly nice accommodations at reasonable rates and with the right attitude. These accommodations are from north to south. **Note:** Hotel prices are quoted in U.S. dollars, since foreign passport holders are exempt from VAT when paying in foreign currency; unless otherwise noted, breakfast is included. If prices are quoted in NIS, inquire about the VAT policy:

- **Almog Kibbutz Holiday Villages** NORTH DEAD SEA—The closest accommodations to Jerusalem, only 25 minutes away. Suitable for couples and small families. ☎ *02/994-5201. www.kibbutz.co.il. Doubles $128–$156.*
- **Kalia Kibbutz Holiday Village** NORTH DEAD SEA—The country lodging section of this kibbutz hotel has upgraded units and can sleep a family. A nice, uncrowded swimming pool. ☎ *02/994-2833. www.kibbutz.co.il. Doubles $102.*
- **Ein Gedi–Beit Sarah Guest House** CENTRAL DEAD SEA—In the same mold as the Rabin and Agron Guest Houses in Jerusalem. Excellent value. ☎ *08/658-4165. www.iyha.org.il. Doubles NIS 394.*
- **Ein Gedi Country Hotel** CENTRAL DEAD SEA—The largest of the area's kibbutz hotels; try for a unit in the Arugot complex, or at least in the Desert category (avoid the Botanical Garden rooms). By far the best food; eat here, even if you do not stay here. ☎ *08/659-4222. www.ein-gedi.co.il. Doubles $175–$224.*
- **Massada Guest House** CENTRAL DEAD SEA—Located right at the foot of Masada, this is a twin of the Ein Gedi–Beit Sarah Guest House, with one superb advantage: a lovely swimming pool, with kiddie area. ☎ *08/658/4349. www.iyha.org.il. Doubles NIS 427.*
- **At Belfer in Neot Hakikar** SOUTH DEAD SEA—The nicest (and roomiest) place to stay, but quite a bit south (at the tip of the sea). Guests stay in cottages with lofts that have double bathtubs with whirlpools. Pick your own breakfast from the Belfers' organic garden. ☎ *052/545-0970. Doubles NIS 400.*

🕐 2–3 hr. Ein Gedi National Park. ☎ 08/658-4285. www.parks.org.il. Antiquities Park admission NIS 13 adults, NIS 7 children; Nature Reserve admission NIS 25 adults, NIS 13 children; no combined ticket available. Daily Oct–Mar 8am–4pm, Apr–Sept 8am–5pm.

④ **Ahava Visitors' Center.**
While Ahava health and beauty

products are sold at factory outlets in Jerusalem, Ein Bokek, and Masada, it is interesting to stop in at the manufacturing plant and view the video that explains the history and benefits of Dead Sea minerals. The sales clerks are very helpful and encourage you to try out a whole range of creams and lotions. ⏱ *20 min. Mitzpeh Shalem.* ☎ *02/994-5117. Sun–Thurs 8am–5pm, Fri 8am–4pm, Sat & holidays 8:30am–5pm.*

⑤ ★ **Enot Tsukim Nature Reserve.** If you are traveling with small children or picnicking, this park is a good choice: The natural streams have been channeled into pools of varying depths for all ages, and there are pleasant picnic tables under shady trees. Maps and suggested trail routes are included in the admission fee. ⏱ *1 hr. Enot Tsukim.* ☎ *02/994-2355. www.parks. org.il. Admission NIS 25 adults, NIS 13 children; a combined ticket to Qumran & Enot Tsukim national parks is available for NIS 36 adults, NIS 18 children. Daily Oct–Mar 8am–5pm, Apr–Sept 8am–4pm.*

⑥ ★★ **Qumran.** The caves in the hills behind the present-day archaeological excavations have yielded amazing treasure troves: mysterious and beautiful copper ritual objects used thousands of years ago by a prehistoric civilization; parchment scrolls of the oldest existing copies of the Torah and other parts of the Bible; even personal letters and artifacts from the Jews' revolts against Rome in the first and second centuries. Who knows what other undiscovered treasures—perhaps the holiest golden relics from King Solomon's Temple—still remain hidden in these vaults of nature? At the national park, you can peer into the closest and most accessible cave, just like the ones where the Dead Sea Scrolls were found in 1947, after viewing the "scriptorium" of

A cave at Qumran.

the sect that still confounds scholars. Don't miss the video presentation in the visitors' center. There is also an air-conditioned restaurant and snack bar. ⏱ *1 hr. Qumran National Park.* ☎ *02/994-2235. www.parks.org.il. Admission NIS 20 adults, NIS 9 children; a combined ticket to Qumran & Enot Tsukim national parks is available for NIS 36 adults, NIS 18 children. Oct–Mar daily 8am–4pm; Apr–Sept daily 8am–5pm.*

⑦ ★★ **Inn of the Good Samaritan.** Along the Jerusalem–Jericho Road is a new museum, opened in 2009, situated inside the 19th-century Turkish caravanserai that was given the name the Inn of the Good Samaritan by some Christian believers. There has been more than a little controversy over this museum since the authorities decided to display mosaics and archaeological findings from Jewish and Samaritan synagogues from all over the country in a facility with a name that reflects predominantly Christian interest. There are, of course, mosaics from ancient churches, plus remnants from the reconstructed Good Samaritan Byzantine Church. The museum can also be visited during the course of a day's sightseeing in and around Jerusalem. ⏱ *45 min. Km 18 on the Jerusalem–Jericho Rd.* ☎ *02/541-7555, Free admission. Sun–Thurs 9am–3pm.*

Tel Aviv & Jaffa in 1 Day

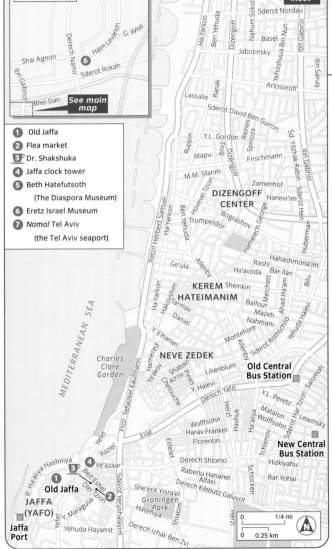

```
0        1/2 mi
0      0.5 km
```

5

Area of inset

See main map

1 Old Jaffa
2 Flea market
3 Dr. Shakshuka
4 Jaffa clock tower
5 Beth Hatefutsoth
   (The Diaspora Museum)
6 Eretz Israel Museum
7 *Namal* Tel Aviv
   (the Tel Aviv seaport)

Jerusalem might be the political and religious capital of Israel, but the "Big Orange" is the country's financial, cultural, and culinary capital. It also has a few of the things that some people look for on vacation (and that Jerusalem lacks), including sandy beaches and non-stop nightlife. And it is all less than an hour away from the Holy City. You can pop down for a quick dip in the Mediterranean and a beer on the boardwalk, spend a whole day in museums or the flea market, or dance the night away in one of the massive hangars-turned-discos at the Tel Aviv seaport. For this tour, we focus on the city's history and culture. START: **Old Jaffa.**

1 ★★ **Old Jaffa.** Jaffa (aka Yafo), populated largely by Christian and Muslim Arabs, has long been the neglected little sister of predominantly Jewish Tel Aviv, which celebrated its 100th birthday in 2009—a drop in the historical bucket compared to the port city of Jaffa, where the armies of the Greeks, the Crusaders, and even Napoleon landed over the centuries. The redesign and reconstruction of ancient Jaffa centers around Kedumim Square, with the imposing church and steeple of the Franciscan Monastery of Saint Peter on the west and a green area with archaeological excavations (including a 5,000-year-old catacomb and an Egyptian gate) to the east. The hilltop park, Gan HaPisgah, contains a white monument depicting scenes from the Bible and slopes northward. The south side of the reclaimed area comprises a maze of alleys, named after the signs of the zodiac and lined with the studios and galleries of some of Israel's leading artists. Old Jaffa is tastefully lit in the evenings; concerts are frequently held here in the summer. Before leaving, make sure you walk near the sea for a view of the curving shoreline and skyline of modern Tel Aviv. Kedumim Plaza, which lies just uphill from Mifratz Shlomo Street, contains the Jaffa Visitor Center, which gives out free, detailed maps of Old Jaffa (with historical information) that make a self-guided tour simple. 🕐 *1 hr.* ☎ *03/682-6796 (visitor center). Bus 10, 46.*

A view of Old Jaffa from the sea.

Getting There

Most Israelis travel between Jerusalem and Tel Aviv by bus or a minivan called a sherut (like the Nesher minivan shuttles that serve the airport from Jerusalem). Express Egged buses depart from Jerusalem's Central Bus Station every 15 minutes to two different terminals: The 405 goes to the Tel Aviv Central Bus Station (better for Jaffa and downtown), while the 480 goes to Tel Aviv's Central Train Station (better for the beach and nightlife). The fare is only NIS 20 each way, so unless you need to make stops on the way, it is both easier and cheaper to use buses and cabs than to rent a car. If you're traveling as a family, or want to relax comfortably and read or use your laptop, consider taking the comparably priced train (from Malha Station; www.rail.co.il/en). It takes a little longer, but if you avoid one traffic jam, you've made up the time; and the scenery is nicer, especially in January, during almond blossom time. For getting around the city on public transport, consult the website of Dan Bus Lines, www.dan.co.il/english. Dan also offers a 2-hour hop-on/hop-off city tour.

❷ ★ **Flea market.** Inland from the reconstituted Old Jaffa complex and seaport is a warren of streets that constitutes the country's largest flea market, which operates year-round. There are scores of historical and artistic items here, but only aficionados of shopping and antiquing will enjoy spending any length of time here. ⏱ *30 min. Between Beit Eshel & Olei Zion sts. Sun–Fri during daylight hr.; closed Sat. Bus: 10, 46, 25.*

A highlight of any visit to Jaffa is a meal at ❸ ★★ **Dr. Shakshuka,** the acknowledged master of the Tripoli tan omelet-like egg-and-tomato dish for which the restaurant is named. The breakfast favorite during Israeli winters is served in individual skillets here, with a whole loaf of fresh bread used to sop up every last drop of the tasty sauce. If you are a party of more than one, order some of the

other North African specialties served here and share. Since the restaurant is kosher, Dr. Shakshuka is closed Friday night and Saturday during the day. *4 Beit Eshel St. ☎ 03/518-6560. $$.*

❹ **Jaffa clock tower.** Located in the Yefet Street Square next to Dr. Shakshuka is one of Jaffa's best known landmarks: the clock tower

Dining at Dr. Shakshuka.

The boardwalk at Namal Tel Aviv.

built by the Sultan of Turkey in 1904. The four clocks at the top used to tell the time in the different time zones in the Ottoman Empire. *Intersection of Yefet & Raziel sts. Bus: 10, 46.*

5 ★★★ kids **Beth Hatefutsoth (The Diaspora Museum).** The Nahum Goldmann Museum of the Jewish Diaspora (conceived by the founder and first president of the World Jewish Congress) is an international museum of the Jewish people through time (history) and space (geography). Hundreds of communities from every corner of the Earth and over two millennia are documented in multimedia exhibits and fascinating scale models. In addition to the massive collections of archival films and Jewish music, high-tech computers are placed at visitors' disposal to search for information about family names and ancestral hometowns. Public transportation is convenient; parking is at the Botanical Garden lot. ⏲ *1.5 hr. Tel Aviv University campus, off Klausner St. inside the Matatia Gate (Gate 2).* ☎ *03/640-8000. www.bh.org.il. Sun–Tues & Thurs 10am–4pm, Wed 10am–6pm, Fri 9am–1pm. Admission (includes audio guide) NIS 35 adults, NIS 25 students & seniors; children under 5 free. AE, DC, MC, V. Bus: 25.*

6 ★★ kids **Eretz Israel Museum.** If the Israel Museum is of the entire history of Jewish culture, and Beth Hatefutsoth is of the

Jewish people outside the land of Israel, this is the museum of Israel the country. The museum complex comprises eight pavilions and an actual *tel*—Tel Qasile, an ancient mound in which 12 strata of past civilizations have been uncovered, including a rebuilt typical house from the pre-Israelite Canaanite period. There is a numismatic pavilion containing rare coins; a glass pavilion with Israel's largest collection of ancient glass; a ceramics pavilion dedicated to the craft of pottery; an ethnography and folklore pavilion of Jewish ethnic art and handicrafts; and even a mining and metallurgy pavilion reminiscent of the legendary King Solomon's mines. ***Tip:*** The Museum Gift Shop is an excellent place to buy interesting souvenirs and presents. ⏲ *1 hr. 2 Chaim Levanon St., Ramat Aviv.* ☎ *03/641-5244. www.eretzmuseum. org.il. Admission NIS 38 adults, NIS 26 students. Sun–Wed 10am–4pm, Thurs 10am–8pm, Fri & Sat 10am–2pm. Bus: 12, 27.*

7 ★★ kids **Namal Tel Aviv.** A good way to end the day is to walk along the boardwalk of the Tel Aviv seaport, a new complex of shops and restaurants along the beach of northern Tel Aviv. There are street entertainers for the children and restaurants of all types (and price ranges). ⏲ *45 min. The entrance to the port area is just east of the corner of Hayarkon & Nahshon sts. Bus: 5.*

Tel Aviv & Jaffa in 2 Days

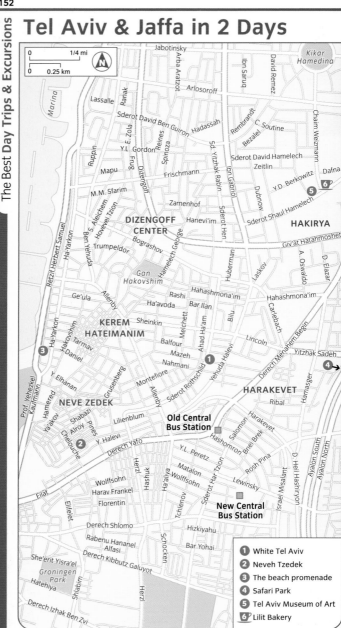

0   1/4 mi
0   0.25 km

Jabotinsky
Arba Aratzot
Arlosoroff
Kikar Hamedina
Ibn Saruq
David Remez
Lassalle
Ranak
Sderot David Ben Guiron
Hadassah
Rembrandt
C. Soutine
Bezalel
Chaim Weizmann
Reines
Spinoza
Y.L. Gordon
E. Zola
Frug
Dizengoff
Frischmann
Sd. Yitzhak Rabin
Ibn Gabirol
Sderot David Hamelech
Zeitlin
Y.D. Berkowitz
Dafna
Mapu
Ruppin
M.M. Sfarim
Zamenhof
Dubnow
Sderot Shaul Hamelech
DIZENGOFF CENTER
Hanevi'im
Sderot Hen
HAKIRYA
S. Aleichem
Hovevei Tzion
Ben Yehuda
Hamelech George
Bograshov
Giv'at Hatahmoshet
Trumpeldor
A. Oswaldo
D. Elazar
Retzif Herbert Samuel
Ha'Yarkon
Gan Hakovshim
Huberman
Laskov
Ge'ula
Allenby
Rashi
Ha'avoda
Hahashmona'im
Hahashmona'im
Carlebach
Ha'Yarkon
Hakovshim
Tarmav
H.Daniel
Sheinkin
Bar Ilan
Bilu
Melchett
Ahad Ha'am
Lincoln
Derech Menahem Begin
Yitzhak Sadeh
KEREM HATEIMANIM
Balfour
Mazeh
Nahmani
Yehuda Halevi
Hamasger
Y. Elhanan
Montefiore
Grusenberg
Allenby
Sderot Rothschild
HARAKEVET
Prof. Yehezkel Kaufmann
Hamered
Ya'akov
Shabazi
Alroy
Pines
Lilienblum
Ribal
NEVE ZEDEK
Chelouche
Y. Halevi
Old Central Bus Station
Salomon
Harakevet
Eilat
Elielet
Derech Yafo
Herzl
Hashuk
Ha'aliya
Y.L. Peretz
Hashomron
Bnei Brek
Rosh Pina
D. Hell Hashinyon
Ayalon South
Ayalon North
Wolffsohn
Matalon
Wolffsohn
Sderot Har Tzion
Lewinsky
Israel Misalant
Harav Frankel
Tchlenov
New Central Bus Station
Florentin
Derech Shlomo
Hizkiyahu
Rabenu Hananel
Alfasi
Derech Kibbutz Galuyot
Bar Yohai
She'erit Yisra'el
Groningen Park
Hatehiya
Schocken
Shlabim
Herzl
Derech Izhak Ben Zvi

1 White Tel Aviv
2 Neveh Tzedek
3 The beach promenade
4 Safari Park
5 Tel Aviv Museum of Art
6 Lilit Bakery

Our second day in Tel Aviv features leisurely strolls through the city's most interesting neighborhoods, or along the beach, where stops can be made for swimming. While the first day's museums focus on history and culture, today the emphasis is on art. START: **Habimah Square, Rothschild Blvd.**

1 ★ **White Tel Aviv.** The city takes great pride in its Bauhaus architecture, accorded UNESCO World Heritage status; the finest examples are on display along Rothschild Boulevard, between the Mann Auditorium–Habimah Theater cultural complex (home to the Israel Philharmonic) and the downtown financial district (anchored by the aging Shalom Tower, once the tallest skyscraper in the Middle East). There is a pedestrian walkway down the middle of the median for the convenience of sightseers. Watch the markings for the parallel bicycle path. ⏱ *1 hr. From Habima Theater Plaza to Nahalat Binyamin St. Bus: 5.*

2 ★ **Neveh Tzedek.** This charming neighborhood has become Tel Aviv's "in" section for the arts, fashion and jewelry designers, and chic restaurants. Meander down the narrow, boutique-lined streets towards (and back from) the highly regarded Suzanne Dallal Centre for Dance and Theatre (between Shabzi and Yehieli sts.); established in 1989, it was the catalyst for the renewal of the rundown neighborhood. ⏱ *1 hr.*

Bounded by Pines St., Neve Shalom St., & Amzaleg St. Bus: 10.

3 ★★ **The beach promenade.** The paved "boardwalk" running along the city's beaches on one side and leading hotels on the other begins at the border between Tel Aviv and Jaffa, and extends practically to the seaport. *Tip:* It is always advisable to swim in the areas supervised by lifeguards, who are on duty from April through October. Simply spread a towel or blanket on the white sand, or rent a comfortable beach recliner for NIS 20 for the whole day. Sections of the promenade are named after (a former British governor) Herbert Samuel (1870–1963) and (ex-mayor) Shlomo Lahat (1927–). *Runs parallel to (& just west of) Hayarkon St., from the Charles Clore Garden to Independence Park. Bus: 8.*

4 ★ kids **Safari Park.** If you have never been to a safari-style animal park or the kids need a change of pace, this is an excellent and exciting example of the genre—and the largest zoological center in the Middle East. In addition to the

Neveh Tzedek is one of the most fashionable neighborhoods in Tel Aviv.

Where to Eat: Israel's Best Restaurants

A reason in itself to come to Tel Aviv is to indulge at one or more of the country's finest dining establishments. Here are a few of the crème de la crème, all meriting this guide's highest star ratings—and priced accordingly (in alphabetical order):

- **Cordelia.** Of the two best French restaurants in Jaffa, the elegant decor in this centuries-old Crusader-era building is as impressive as the adventuresome menu, which has been called "food as theater." Chef Nir Zook also presides over the nearby Noa Bistro, a good choice if Cordelia is booked (or you want to spend a tad less). *30 Yefet St., near the clock tower.* ☎ *03/ 518-4668. Entrees NIS 80–NIS 130. AE, DC, MC, V. Lunch & dinner Mon–Sat.*

- **Herbert Samuel.** Chef Jonathan Roshfeld's sumptuously glossy cookbooks are on display—as are the workings of the kitchens—in this popular restaurant overlooking the Mediterranean in the seam between Tel Aviv and Jaffa. *Tapas*-sized portions are available for some of the offerings. *6 Kaufman St., Beit Gibor.* ☎ *03/516-6516. NIS 79–99. AE, DC, MC, V. Lunch & dinner Mon–Sat.*

- **Lilit.** The only kosher choice on our list of the best of Tel Aviv, Lilit is admired both for its cuisine and unique project for the benefit of society: It employs youth at risk, training them for a good career in the culinary arts. The restaurant employs a full-time social worker to ensure the program is on track; the results point to resounding success. Ask about discounted "business lunches," which include an appetizer for the price of just the entree. *4 Weizmann St.* ☎ *03/609-1331. Entrees NIS 59–NIS 150. AE, DC, MC, V. Lunch & dinner Sun–Thurs; closed Fri & Sat.*

- **Raphael.** Chef Rafi Cohen presents French Mediterranean–Israeli fusion cuisine in his sleekly modern restaurant overlooking the beach promenade and the water. The food is distracting enough from the noise of a crowded dining room, but if you prefer relative quiet, come before 9pm. *87 Hayarkon St. (adjacent to the Dan Hotel).* ☎ *03/522-6464. Entrees NIS 100–NIS 150. AE, DC, MC, V. Lunch & dinner daily.*

free-roaming hippos, lions, elephants, rhinos, and giraffes, there is a monkey enclosure, an aviary, and a reptile area. ⏱ *2 hr. Ramat Gan.* ☎ *03/631-3531. www.safari.co.il. Sat–Thurs & holidays Sept–June* *9am–4pm, July & Aug 9am–5pm; Fri year-round 9am–1pm. Admission NIS 49 adults, NIS 42 students & seniors; additional NIS 7 charge for Safaribus if you don't have a car. Bus: 67.*

Where to Sleep

Unlike Jerusalem, many of the leading international hotel chains are represented in this cosmopolitan city. My favorite, however, is a relatively new boutique hotel just 2 blocks from the Tel Aviv seaport: the Port Hotel, the latest from the Sun chain of Tel Aviv boutique hotels. The rooftop terrace is like being on the beach without the hassle. *288 Hayarkon St. (corner of 4 Yirmiyahu St.).* ☎ *03/544-5544. www.porthoteltelaviv.com. Doubles $130.*

Other recommended, affordable options are the Mishkenot Ruth Daniel Guest House, conveniently located near both Old Jaffa and the beach promenade (☎ 03/682-7700, www.iyha.org.il), and the Bnei Dan Guest House, in the pastoral Yarkon River Park section of Tel Aviv (☎ 03/594-5655, www.iyha.org.il). *Doubles NIS 394–NIS 398 for both guest houses.*

If money is no object, the Dan Tel Aviv Hotel is Tel Aviv's equivalent of the King David in Jerusalem (see p 137). Located on the beach in the heart of the city, the only Tel Aviv member of the exclusive international association Leading Hotels of the World features posh rooms, whirlpool spas, and a pleasant business lounge. *87 Hayarkon St.* ☎ *03/520-2552. www.danhotels.com. Doubles $360–$990.*

⑤ Tel Aviv Museum of Art. The city's main cultural complex, named after Israel's American-raised Prime Minister Golda Meir (1898–1978), comprises the Center for Performing Arts, the Opera

The cultural complex home to the Tel Aviv Museum of Art.

House, the Cameri Theater, and the Tel Aviv Museum of Art. The latter houses a world-class collection of Impressionist and post-Impressionist art. 🕐 *1½ hr. 27 Shaul Hamelech Blvd.* ☎ *03/607-7020. www.ta museum.com. Admission NIS 45 adults (includes admission to Helena Rubinstein Pavilion for Contemporary Art). Mon, Wed & Sat 10am–4pm; Tues & Thurs 10am–10pm; Fri 10am–2pm & 7–10pm. Bus: 38, 149.*

The popular Lilit Restaurant (see sidebar, p 154) has recently opened the **⑥ Lilit Bakery,** which serves up a delicious variety of baked goods that cannot be served in the restaurant proper (where no food can contain dairy products). And here you can have milk in your coffee. *4 Weizmann St.* ☎ *03/609-1331. $.*

The Jerusalem Corridor

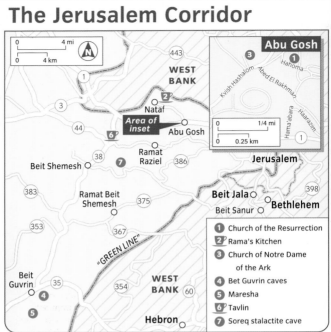

1 Church of the Resurrection
2 Rama's Kitchen
3 Church of Notre Dame of the Ark
4 Bet Guvrin caves
5 Maresha
6 Tavlin
7 Soreq stalactite cave

The foothills lying between ancient Philistine territory and Jerusalem contain caves of both natural beauty and historical significance dating back to the days of David and Goliath. Closer to the capital, the Biblical Kiryat Ye'arim is now the modern village of Abu Gosh, populated primarily by Christian Arabs who have been remarkably loyal to the State of Israel since the 1948 War of Independence. Jerusalemites flock here on Saturdays to enjoy hummus and other Middle Eastern favorites in the town's numerous restaurants. START: **Rte. 1 leading west out of Jerusalem.**

1 ★ **Church of the Resurrection.** This 12th-century Crusader treasure is situated on top of an ancient cistern that was in use from early Canaanite times. Now under the guardianship of France's Lazarist fathers, the sanctuary has marvelous acoustics for Gregorian chants. *Intersection of Haj Musa Rd. & Hahoma St. Free admission. Mon–Wed, Fri & Sat 8:30–11:30am & 2:30–5:30pm.*

The delicious appetizers, taboun-baked flatbreads, and desserts served up in 2 ★★ **Rama's Kitchen** are only part of the attraction; the view of Israel's entire coastal plain is spectacular. The rustic atmosphere comes complete with dogs wandering in and out. *Nataf, a Jewish settlement just up the hill from Abu Gosh.* ☎ *02/570-0954. $$$.*

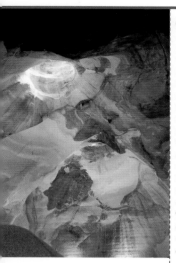

The bell-shaped cavern within the Bet Guvrin Caves.

5 ★★ kids **Maresha.** The inhabitants of this former capital of the province of Idumea were forced (in the second century BCE) either to become Jews or leave. No one could have imagined that the grandson of one of these forced converts would be none other than the notorious King Herod. One of the most underrated historical sites in all of Israel, this underground city is home to an amazing columbarium (an ancient dovecote housing birds kept for ritual purposes), as well as the skillfully decorated Sidonian Tombs. *Bet Guvrin–Maresha National Park.* ☎ *08/681-2957. Admission (includes entrance to both Maresha & Bet Guvrin, above) NIS 25 adults, NIS 13 children. Daily 8:30am–3pm.*

3 Church of Notre Dame of the Ark. This house of worship was erected on the site where a Byzantine church is thought to have marked the last stop of the Ark of the Covenant before it was brought to Jerusalem by King David. Crowned by a majestic statue of the Madonna holding the baby Jesus, the church is another of the concert venues of the town's semi-annual festivals of sacred music. *Hilltop overlooking Abu Gosh. Free admission. Daily 8:30–11:30am & 2:30–5:30pm.*

4 ★ kids **Bet Guvrin caves.** The centerpiece of this network of caves in the soft, chalky limestone soil is a huge bell-shaped cavern whose natural acoustics make it an unforgettable venue for choral performances—or wedding receptions when floodlit at night. *Bet Guvrin–Maresha National Park.* ☎ *08/681-2957. Admission (includes entrance to both Bet Guvrin & Maresha, below) NIS 25 adults, NIS 13 children. Daily 8:30am–3pm.*

The pleasant restaurant at **6** **Tavlin** is actually secondary to the large spice and gifts emporium that draws shoppers from both Jerusalem and Tel Aviv. It gets very crowded on weekends. *Eshtaol, next to the Flam Winery (see p 159).* ☎ *02/992-4995. $$.*

7 ★ kids **Soreq stalactite cave.** The stalactite formations in this cave delight children and adults alike. An informative video presentation explains the geology behind the phenomenon. *Avshalom Nature Reserve.* ☎ *02/991-1117. Admission NIS 25 adults, NIS 13 children. Sat–Thurs 8:30am–3pm, Fri 8:30am–2pm.*

Judean Hills Wineries

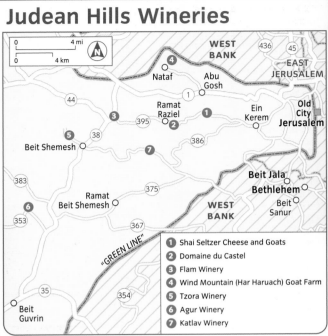

1. Shai Seltzer Cheese and Goats
2. Domaine du Castel
3. Flam Winery
4. Wind Mountain (Har Haruach) Goat Farm
5. Tzora Winery
6. Agur Winery
7. Katlav Winery

The hills leading up to Jerusalem from Israel's coastal plain are rich in history (the battles between the Israelites and Philistines were fought here, as well as key skirmishes in the 1948 War of Independence) and natural beauty. More recently, the area has become home to some 30 wineries reviving one of mankind's earliest industries, complemented by artisan cheese makers who still pasture their goats in the manner of their Biblical ancestors.

START: **Rte. 1 leading west out of Jerusalem.**

---

1 ★★★ Shai Seltzer Cheese and Goats. Universally acknowledged as the finest cheese maker in Israel, Seltzer is frequently called upon to judge goat cheese contests in Italy and France. Like many artists, Seltzer is a bit eccentric: He sells his award-winning cheeses only to those who make a weekend pilgrimage to his farm. An outing here is lovely and tasty, but does not come cheap: His best cheeses can cost up to $40 a pound! The varieties range from mild soft cheeses to pungent aged wheels with exotic rinds made of cured vine leaves and crushed grape seeds. *Har Eitan Farm, Sataf.* ☎ *02/533-3748. www.goat-cheese.co.il. Sat 11am–4pm; variable hr. on Fri (call first).*

② ★★ **Domaine du Castel.** One of the pioneers of the contemporary generation of wineries is Domaine du Castel, which has had vintages scored above 90 by noted wine critic Robert Parker. The owners are prime movers for the recognition of the Judean Hills as an official *terroir*. Castel offers tours of its cellar, but you must strictly follow the guides' instructions, so as not to jeopardize its kosher status. *Ramat Raziel.* ☎ *02/534-2249. www.castel.co.il.*

③ ★★★ **Flam Winery.** A thoroughly modern winery that uses grapes from throughout the country to make its wines in the tradition of Italy. *Eshtaol.* ☎ *02/992-9923. Tastings NIS 60 per person (for five wines), NIS 100 with assorted cheeses. Sun–Fri by appointment only; specify the number in your party.*

④ ★ 🔲 **kids Wind Mountain (Har Haruach) Goat Farm.** The Himmelfarb family farm produces a variety of creamy and semi-soft goat cheeses, including one slightly aged in grape leaves. They also make goats' milk yogurt and seasonal jams. Families might consider getting the picnic basket special. Parents take note: The

The Domaine du Castel is one Israel's pioneering wineries.

goats return from grazing every afternoon around 3pm; children are invited to pet them and perhaps participate in the milking. *Nataf 35, at the turnoff to the Memorial Forest for the Jews of Poland.* ☎ *02/534-5660.*

The cheese at Shai Seltzer is universally acknowledged as Israel's best.

Driving Trip Planner

Driving rural Israel's winding, narrow roads presents its challenges. If you want a longer self-guided itinerary mapped out in detail, **Drive Israel** (☎ 646/240-4334 in the U.S. or 050/771-3823; www.drive-israel.com) can customize routes, directions, and points of interest along the way, as well as handle reservations for accommodations and restaurants.

www.harharuach.com. Fri 10am–4pm, Sat 10am–5pm.

5 ★★ kids **Tzora Winery.** This kosher winery is located on a kibbutz close to the city of Beit Shemesh, where the Judean Hills meet the coastal plain. There is a pleasant picnic area on the premises, right outside a shop selling wine, cheese, and other gourmet items. Saturdays can get crowded. *Kibbutz Tzora.* ☎ 02/990-8261. www.tzoravineyards. com. *Tasting fee NIS 15 (for three wines), refunded upon your purchase. Sun–Thurs 9am–5pm, Fri 9am–2pm, Sat 10am–5pm.*

6 ★★ **Agur Winery.** A kosher winery with a growing reputation; tastings are held in a bohemian outdoor setting. *Moshav Agur.* ☎ 02/999-5423. *Tasting fee NIS 20 (refundable upon purchase). Fri & Sat 10am–4pm & by appointment.*

7 ★ **Katlav Winery.** A kosher winery founded by a well-known architect who gave up his profession to follow his passion for winemaking. Tastings and banquets (by prior arrangement) are held in its rustic surroundings. *Ness Harim.* ☎ 02/570-3575. www.katlav.co.il. *Tasting fees NIS 50–NIS 90.* ●

Katlav is a kosher winery founded by a well-known architect.

The
Savvy Traveler

Before You Go

Israel Government Tourist Offices

In the United States: 800 Second Ave., New York, NY 10117; ☎ 212/499-5650; 6380 Wilshire Blvd., Ste. 1718, Los Angeles, CA 90048; ☎ 323/658-7463.

In Canada: 180 Bloor St. W., Ste. 700, Toronto, ON M5S 2V6; ☎ 416/964-3784.

In the U.K. & Ireland: UK House 180 Oxford Street, London W1D 1NN; ☎ 20/7299-1111.

The Best Times to Go

Most visitors come to Israel during the summer vacation months, and to celebrate religious holidays. Needless to say, both airfares and hotel prices are significantly higher during these times. The summers are hot, however; see **Weather** (p 163).

The best times to visit, therefore, are in the autumn and spring, when there are fewer crowds (with the exception of the Jewish holidays of Passover in spring and Sukkot in fall) and the weather is most conducive to sightseeing. Winters in Jerusalem can be chilly, although one can escape the cold at the Dead Sea or even Tel Aviv.

You are most likely to encounter rain between November and March, but rarely for more than 1-2 days at a time. Jerusalem is in the Judean Hills, so it is advisable to pack a sweater or jacket for the evenings, even in summer.

Some holidays that are fun in Israel are Purim (usually March) and Independence Day (generally May).

Festivals, Holidays & Special Events

WINTER—A relatively recent tradition is **"Long Nights"—Hot Winter**

in Jerusalem (☎ 02/531-4600 in Hebrew; www.jerusalem.muni.il): Three long December weekends of events, exhibitions, musical performances, and free tours of the city are offered. Most museums offer specially discounted admission. Every December, the Jerusalem Cinematheque hosts a **Jewish Film Festival** (☎ 02/565-4333; www.jer-cin.org.il), featuring entries from around the world. Jerusalem's biennial **International Book Fair** (☎ 02/629-6415; www.jerusalembookfair.com), held in February of odd-numbered years, is beginning to rival Frankfurt's in prestige.

SPRING—Recalling how Queen Esther saved her people in Persia in the 5th century BCE, **Purim (Feast of Lots)** is an exciting time when folks, especially children, dress up in fancy or zany (or sometimes irreligious) costumes, have parties, parade in the streets, give food baskets, spray shaving cream at passersby, and generally make merry. In Jerusalem, Purim (which falls in the Hebrew month of Adar) is celebrated 1 day later than in the rest of the country. Israel's **Independence Day** falls in April or May (corresponding to the 5th day of the Hebrew month of Iyar) and is marked by Israeli dancing in the streets and fireworks in the evening. **Jerusalem Day** marks the anniversary of the reunification of the city in May 1967. The date varies from year to year because the holiday is fixed according to the Hebrew date of 28 Iyar. National celebrities perform in honor of the city. (For information on Jerusalem Day events, ☎ 02/531-4600 in Hebrew; www.jerusalem.muni.il.)

SUMMER—The annual month-long **Israel Festival** (☎ 02/566-3198;

www.festival.co.il) showcases the world's greatest musical, theatrical, and dance artists every June and is considered a leading international cultural event. The **Jerusalem Film Festival** (☎ 02/565-4333; www.jff. org.il), held annually in June, is an international festival of increasing renown. It is modeled after the Cannes, Venice, and Berlin festivals, so films do not necessarily revolve around Jewish themes.

Each August, the Hutzot Hayo-tzer artists' complex at the foot of the Old City walls plays host to **The International Arts and Crafts Fair** (☎ 02/531-4600 in Hebrew; www. jerusalem.muni.il). More than 150 artists representing some 50 countries display their wares. For 25 years, Jerusalem has been one of the hosts of **The International Festival of Puppet Theaters** (☎ 02/561-8514; www.traintheater.co.il). Hardly a day in August goes by without an entertaining performance. Food and drink are celebrated, as well: A **Wine Festival** is held at the Israel Museum in July, and **The Art and Pasta Festival** (☎ 02/531-4600 in Hebrew; www.jerusalem. muni.il) at the Museum of Italian Jewish Art in August.

FALL—Music takes center stage in the autumn, with the **Jerusalem International Festival of Chamber Music** (☎ 02/625-0444; www.

jcmf.org.il) in September and the **International Oud Festival** (☎ 02/531-4600 in Hebrew; www.jerusalem. muni.il) in November, dedicated to the art of the Middle Eastern lute.

The Weather

Israel has a Mediterranean climate, but Jerusalem's climate is affected by its Judean Hills' altitude. In general, summers are very hot in the daytime and somewhat cool in the evenings; it is rare to encounter rain in the summer months. Winters are cold and can be rainy, with the occasional snowfall. As a general rule, mid-April to mid-June and mid-September to early November are the ideal times to visit, from the point of view of moderate temperatures. Detailed local weather can be checked at www.02ws.com.

Cellphones (Mobile Phones)

U.S. CDMA cellphones will not work in Israel, which operates on the GSM system. Check with your service provider to find out what kind of phone you have. Cellphones can be readily rented either at Israel's Ben-Gurion Airport, in Jerusalem, or before you leave home. One company with toll-free numbers in several countries is **IsraelPhones** (☎ 866/897-9393 in the U.S.; 800/721-111 in Israel; 800/404-9642 in the U.K.; 866/302-5512 in Canada; 800/076-284 in Australia; www.israelphones.com).

JERUSALEM AVERAGE HIGH & LOW TEMPERATURE (°F & °C) & MONTHLY RAINFALL (INCHES)

	JAN	FEB	MAR	APR	MAY	JUNE
Temp (°F)	53/43	57/44	61/47	69/53	77/60	81/66
Temp (°C)	12/6	14/7	16/8	21/12	25/16	27/19
Rainfall (in.)	5.6	4.5	3.9	1.2	0.1	0.0

	JULY	AUG	SEPT	OCT	NOV	DEC
Temp (°F)	84/66	86/66	82/65	78/60	67/54	56/47
Temp (°C)	29/19	30/19	28/18	26/16	19/12	13/8
Rainfall (in.)	0.0	0.0	0.0	0.9	2.7	4.3

Getting There

By Plane

Israel is served by most major international air carriers. Israel's flag carrier is **El Al Israel Airlines** (see "Useful Websites," p 176, for contact information for all airlines), which flies to every continent except Australia. U.S. airlines flying directly to Jerusalem's Ben-Gurion International Airport (BGU) include **Continental Airlines, Delta Air Lines,** and **USAirways.** Virtually every U.S. airline connects to Israel via a European partner carrier. Another Israeli airline serving the U.S. is **Israir Airlines.** As this guide went to press, Israel's **Arkia Airlines** was planning to institute flights between the U.S. and Israel.

The best way to get from Ben-Gurion to Jerusalem is via the shared van service operated by Nesher. The vans load at the airport on a first-come, first-served basis and take you directly to the address of your destination. Pay the driver directly in cash, in either U.S. or Israeli currency. The fare is NIS 50 or $15. Tipping is not necessary unless the driver goes out of his way in some fashion. If you do not want to share a van, you may order a taxi from the dispatcher; rates from BGU to all major cities in Israel are fixed. At press time, the fare to Jerusalem was NIS 270.

Nesher operates 24 hours a day, 7 days a week. However, its offices for reserving a return trip to the airport are closed on the Sabbath. Whatever day of the week you are traveling between Jerusalem and BGU, it is highly recommended to book your seats 1 to 2 days in advance.

Getting Around

Car Rental

BGU is served by most major U.S and international car rental companies, but there is an extra fee from renting at the airport; in any event, renting a car is not necessary—and generally not recommended—if you are spending most of your time in the cities of Jerusalem and Tel Aviv. The streets are congested, many road signs are only in Hebrew, and parking is difficult (both in terms of a limited number of spaces and complicated payment procedures). Plus, given the price of gas, it is still cheaper to take taxis several times a day throughout the city than it is to rent a car.

If you still feel the need to rent a vehicle, see "Useful Websites" (p 176); prices per day range from $30-$50. If renting a car for the day trips or excursions described in chapter 9, see p 145.

Public Transportation

Egged (☎ *2800; www.egged.co.il/eng) is the national bus cooperative of Israel, providing inter-city service, as well as urban service in West Jerusalem; the company maintains a very user-friendly website in English for planning trips within and outside of the city. The fare for one bus ride in Jerusalem is NIS 5.90. A pre-paid card *(kartisiya)* of 10 trips saves time, money, and hassles. Taxis are plentiful in the city and easily recognizable by their white color with black markings and yellow rooftop lights. They may be ordered by your

Jerusalem's Light Rail Transformation

As this guide went to press, a good part of downtown Jerusalem was still under construction as part of a long-awaited transformation: Towards the end of 2010, a state-of-the-art light rail system is to replace many of the city's former bus routes. In addition, all of Jaffa Road will become a pedestrian mall. The website for the light rail operating company is http://citypass.co.il/starthomee.html. Your hotel or the Egged website (www.egged.co.il/eng) will also have details of the revamped transit system.

hotel or restaurant, or simply flagged down. Jerusalem taxi drivers are notorious for ripping off tourists: Insist that the driver use the meter (in Hebrew, moan-eh). The starting fare within the city is NIS 11, with an additional charge of NIS 4.10 for telephone orders and NIS 3.40 for each suitcase that is not hand luggage. Night rates (9pm–5:30am) are 25% more than the normal fare; this rate also applies on the Sabbath and holidays. Tipping is not customary unless the driver performs an extra service.

Israel Railways (☎ *5770; http://rakevet.co.il/en) operates comfortable trains linking Jerusalem, Tel Aviv, BGU, Haifa, Beersheba, and points in between. Unfortunately, there is no direct link between BGU and Jerusalem. Moreover, the train station in Jerusalem is far from centrally located, and the journey to Tel Aviv is longer than by bus or *sherut* (shared minivan). Still, it could be advisable if traveling with small children who need space to walk around while traveling.

Fast Facts

AREA CODES—The area codes in use in this guide are 02 for Jerusalem, 03 for Tel Aviv, and 08 for the central and southern areas of the Dead Sea.

BUSINESS HOURS—Banks and post offices are open Sunday to Thursday mornings and some afternoons. Israelis have long ago given up trying to figure out which branches of which banks are open which afternoons and at what hours. It is advisable to take care of your business between 8am and noon. Some banks and post offices are open Friday mornings.

CONSULATES AND EMBASSIES—**Australian Embassy,** 23 Yehuda Halevi St., Tel Aviv (☎ 03/693-5000; www.australianembassy.org.il). **Canadian Embassy,** 3/5 Nirim St., Tel Aviv (☎ 03/636-3300; www.canadainternational.gc.ca/israel). **New Zealand Consulate,** 3 Daniel Frish St., Tel Aviv (☎ 03/695-6622). **United Kingdom Consulate-General, Jerusalem,** 19 Nashashibi St., Jerusalem (☎ 02/541-4100). **United Kingdom Embassy,** 1 Ben Yehuda St., Tel Aviv (☎ 03/510-0166; http://ukinisrael.fco.gov.uk/en). **United**

Useful Websites

- **www.jerusalem.muni.il**—The website of the Jerusalem municipality has useful information under the tabs labeled Visitors, Events, and Tourism.
- **www.goisrael.com**—The official website of the Israel Ministry of Tourism can be helpful, especially in the pre-planning stages of your trip.
- **www.frommers.com**—Your favorite travel guide website often has up-to-date and insider information.
- **www.jerusalem.com**—Once a public sector initiative that has now been privatized, this website references a number of categories of interest. (Take the recommendations with a grain of salt; it never has a bad word to say about anybody.)
- **www.sacred-destinations.com/israel/jerusalem**—A comprehensive resource with interesting details about Jerusalem's many and varied holy sites.
- **www.israel-travel-tips.com**—The English will make you laugh (or cringe), but this native Israeli is sincere in trying to help the visitor understand his country.
- **www.jerusalem-coupons.com**—Your hotel should have the hard-copy version in the lobby; otherwise, print from the website to save a little bit on your next meal.
- **www.jercity.com/eng**—Among other useful information and lifestyle listings, a weekly calendar of events.
- **www.ecotourism-israel.com/Index.htm**—Insights, advice, and recommendations about sustainable tourism in Israel.

States Consulate General, 27 Nablus Rd., Jerusalem (☎ 02/622-7221; 02/622-7207; http://jerusalem. usconsulate.gov). **United States Embassy,** 71 Hayarkon St., Tel Aviv (☎ 03/519-7575; http://usembassy-israel.org.il).

CONVENIENCE (24-HR.) STORES—The **SOS** chain of stores operates four branches in West Jerusalem, clearly identified by their large blue signs. In West Jerusalem, the rule is 24/6; the rabbis have forced the city to close down businesses on the Sabbath. Other convenience stores are open on the Sabbath in East Jerusalem and the Old City.

CONVERTERS AND ADAPTERS—See "Electricity," below.

CURRENCY EXCHANGE—See "Money," below.

DOCTORS AND DENTISTS—For non-emergency medical treatment, **Terem** (☎ 599/520-520) operates several 24-hour clinics providing walk-in care. A number of American doctors practice at the **Wolfson Medical Center** (9 Diskin St.; ☎ 02/563-6265). An English-speaking dentist is **Dr. Stanley Brodie** (2 Marcus St.; ☎ 02/561-0411). Dr. Gene Stollman is an American-trained optometrist who can help if you lose your glasses. His office is shared with an optician (33 Jaffa Road, ☎ 054/456-8791).

DRUGSTORES—See "Pharmacies," below.

ELECTRICITY—The electric current used in Israel is 220 volts AC (50 cycles), as opposed to the 110-volt system used in America. If you bring an electric shaver or hair dryer designed for 110 volts to Israel, you must use a proper transformer to convert the current. Cheap converters are not safe and sooner or later will cause damage. Do not use sensitive electronic items such as computers unless they have internal transformers that automatically convert to both 110 and 220 voltage systems. Sockets (or power points) are designed to accept plugs with either two or three round prongs. If your appliance with the proper voltage still does not have the right plug, you can buy an adapter quite easily and cheaply, or your hotel may have one to lend to you.

EMERGENCIES—For police, dial ☎ **100;** for fire, dial ☎ **102;** for medical emergency/ambulance, dial ☎ **101.**

FAXING AND PHOTOCOPYING—Faxing services are widely available at hotels and post offices. Most hotels also have photocopying machines, as do many establishments in downtown Jerusalem. **Absolut Copy** at 36 Ben Yehuda St. (☎ 02/624-5459) photocopies in black-and-white and color.

HAIRCUTS—Both men and women can get a good haircut at **Signon Ha'eer** (5 Eliash St.; ☎ 077/350-0381).

HOLIDAY OBSERVANCES—Like the Sabbath, Jewish religious holidays begin at sundown and end at sundown on the following day. Many of these holidays carry the same restrictions as the Sabbath, so services like public transportation are curtailed (the Day of Atonement, known as Yom Kippur, is like a super-Sabbath; the whole country basically shuts down). Even Israeli secular holidays are determined by the Hebrew calendar, so they will fall on different Gregorian dates every year. Christmas and New Year's are not observed as public holidays in Israel.

INSURANCE—**Medical Insurance**—Although it's not required of travelers, health insurance is highly recommended. Most health insurance policies cover you if you get sick away from home—but check your coverage before you leave. For travel overseas, most U.S. health plans (including Medicare and Medicaid) do not provide coverage, and the ones that do often require you to pay for services upfront and reimburse you only after you return home. As a safety net, you may want to buy travel medical insurance; one source is **Travel Assistance International** (☎ 800/821-2828; www.travelassistance.com). However, if a U.S. citizen visits a country that's on the State Department warning list, most U.S. health insurance policies are not required to cover them while in said country. This is rarely a problem for Jerusalem, but could be for traveler who go into the West Bank. **Canadians** should check with their provincial health plan offices or contact **Health Canada** (☎ 866/225-0709; www.hc-sc.gc.ca) to find out the extent of their coverage and what documentation and receipts they must take home in case they are treated overseas. Travelers from the U.K. should carry their European Health Insurance Card (EHIC), which replaced the E111 form as proof of entitlement to free/reduced cost medical treatment abroad (☎ 0845/606-2030; www.ehic.org.uk). Note, however, that the EHIC covers only "necessary medical treatment," and for repatriation costs, lost money and baggage, and cancellation coverage, travel insurance from a reputable company should always be sought (www.travelinsuranceweb.com).

Travel Insurance—The cost of travel insurance varies widely, depending on the destination, the cost and length of your trip, your age and health, and the type of trip you're taking, but expect to pay between 5% and 8% of the vacation itself. You can get estimates from various providers through **Insure-MyTrip.com** (www.insuremytrip.com). Enter your trip cost and dates, your age, and other information for prices from more than a dozen companies. U.K. citizens and their families who make more than one trip abroad per year may find an annual travel insurance policy works out cheaper. Check www.money supermarket.com, which compares prices across a wide range of providers for single- and multi-trip policies. Trip cancellation insurance will help retrieve your money if you have to back out of a trip or depart early, or if your travel supplier goes bankrupt. Trip cancellation traditionally covers such events as sickness, natural disasters, and U.S. State Department advisories. For details, contact one of the following recommended insurers: **Access America** (☎ 866/807-3982; www.access america.com), **Travel Guard International** (☎ 800/826-4919; www.travelguard.com), **Travel Insured International** (☎ 800/243-3174; www.travelinsured.com), and **Travelex Insurance Services** (☎ 888/457-4602; www.travelex-insurance.com).

INTERNET ACCESS—For travelers with laptops or handheld devices, many of Jerusalem's downtown coffee shops provide free Wi-Fi Internet service. In addition, cybercafes abound. **Sandeman's Travelers' Center** (in the Zabotinsky bar; 1 Ben Shetah St.; ☎ 02/624-4726) allows you 15 minutes free on one of its two computers until 7pm. Otherwise, expect to pay approximately NIS 15 per hour (proportionally more for shorter periods of time). **Hotel Avital's** (141 Jaffa Rd., near Mahane Yehuda market) entire ground floor is an Internet cafe; **Internet Caffe** (31 Jaffa Rd.) has two floors of computer terminals. In East Jerusalem, try **Old City Net** (Latin Patriarchate Rd., to the left of Jaffa Gate; ☎ 02/627-5799).

LOST PROPERTY—Be sure to inform all of your credit card companies the minute you discover your wallet has been lost or stolen, and file a report at the nearest police station. Credit card companies have an emergency toll-free number to call if your card is lost or stolen; they may be able to wire you a cash advance immediately or deliver an emergency credit card in a day or two. In Israel, the emergency numbers for lost credit cards are as follows: **American Express** (☎ 800/940-3211), **Visa** (☎ 800/941-6384), and **MasterCard** (☎ 800/941-8873).

MAIL AND POSTAGE—The **Israeli Postal Service** (www.israelpost.co.il) is dependable. Postal rates are similar to those in the United States and the U.K. Packages must be brought to the post office unsealed for security inspection, and you must present your passport to the postal clerk.

MONEY—It is not advisable to change money at banks, and even less so at hotels. Legal currency exchange outlets line the Ben Yehuda Street pedestrian mall, Jaffa Road, and King George Street (they offer slightly better rates than banks, will change money in less time, and charge no commission; they also have longer hours). There is no need to shop around: They all offer the same rates. Most post offices will change money at competitive rates. ATMs connected to the major international networks can also be found on the Ben Yehuda mall. A small fee will apply to your withdrawal.

NEWSPAPERS AND MAGAZINES—The English daily edition of *Ha'aretz,* Israel's most respected Hebrew-language newspaper, comes free inside the daily *International Herald Tribune.* The *Jerusalem Post* is Israel's main English-language daily. Newspapers are not published on Saturdays, so the "weekend" edition is the Friday edition.

PALESTINIAN TERRITORIES—Jerusalem is surrounded (except on the west) by the area of land that is known as the West Bank (aka Judea and Samaria), which is controlled by Israel, but some of which is governed by an autonomous entity called the Palestinian Authority (PA). The PA is in charge of Jericho and Bethlehem. While entry to and from the former is uncomplicated (although your rental car insurance may not be valid there), going to Bethlehem is the equivalent of crossing a border: You must present your passport and endure a sometimes lengthy airport-type security screening when returning to Jerusalem. Bethlehem may be reached by both Arab and Jewish city buses (the latter go directly to Rachel's Tomb without crossing the checkpoint). Hassles can be reduced by taking an organized tour, such as those offered by ICAHD (www. icahd.org). See p 23 or Travel Agencies (below, p 170).

PASSPORTS AND VISAS—Foreign visitors to Israel require a valid passport from their country of origin. Citizens of the U.S., Canada, the U.K., Australia, and New Zealand do not require a visa to enter Israel as a tourist for stays up to 3 months.

PHARMACIES—Most pharmacists in Jerusalem speak English, and drugstores generally carry many of the same over-the-counter items as in North America and Europe. A reliable chain of stores is **SuperPharm.**

RELIGIOUS CUSTOMS AND SERVICES—It is always advisable, and only respectful, to dress modestly when visiting houses of worship. Men should wear long pants in mosques, even though they can generally wear shorts in churches and synagogues; women should cover shoulders, cleavage, and thighs not only at holy sites, but in Arab and religious Jewish neighborhoods. A list of church services can be obtained from the Christian Information Center near Jaffa Gate (☎ 02/627-2692). Virtually all of Jerusalem's numerous synagogues follow the Orthodox tradition of segregating men and women into separate seating sections during prayer services. A list of more progressive synagogues, most of which permit mixed seating, can be found at www. kbyonline.org.

SECURITY—Israel is a very security-conscious country; your bags will be inspected when you enter any public facility. People are generally courteous and patient during this procedure.

SMOKING—Smoking is not permitted in any conveyances or indoors in any public places, including cafes, restaurants, and bars (except in specified areas for smokers). This law is sometimes ignored in West Jerusalem and widely ignored in East Jerusalem.

Another Source of Useful Information

The weekend (Friday) edition of the local *Ha'aretz/International Herald Tribune* publishes a supplement called *The Guide*. Following the entertainment and TV listings, on the page opposite the inside back cover, is a helpful list of telephone numbers of various offices and agencies, arranged by familiar categories.

TELEPHONE—Israel's public telephones are mostly for phone cards only. A few public phones take one-shekel coins, and one-shekel coins are needed for pay phones in neighborhood groceries and restaurants. Many convenience stores and newsstands sell prepaid calling cards in denominations ranging from NIS 20 to NIS 100. To reverse charges or make collect calls, and for operator-assisted overseas or person-to-person calls, dial ☎ 188. For local directory assistance ("information"), dial ☎ 144; 700- and 800-numbers are toll-free. Many companies provide a toll-free 4-digit number prefaced with a * that can be dialed from any local telephone. For international calling, the country code for Israel is 972.

TIPPING—Tip 10% to 15% in restaurants or cafes, unless a service charge is already added to your bill. Taxi drivers do not expect tips unless they have helped you load or carry luggage.

TRAVEL AGENCIES—The Association of Americans and Canadians in Israel has designated **Ophir Tours** its official travel agency. A good option for booking international travel, including quick trips to neighboring countries. (42 Agrippas Street, ☎ 539-8666). Domestic bookings can also be made through **Mabat Platinum**, ☎ 03/961-8930 (their Jerusalem specialist is Danby Meital).

WATER—Water is potable throughout Israel, except at the Dead Sea, where bottled water is recommended.

A Brief History of **Jerusalem**

1100–1050 BCE Following the Exodus from Egypt, Israelite tribes settle in Canaan, west of the Jordan River.

1025 BCE The Israelite nation becomes a monarchy; Saul is anointed first king by the prophet Samuel.

1000 BCE David, second Israelite king, conquers Jerusalem and makes the small city his capital.

950 BCE King Solomon builds the First Temple of Jerusalem.

928 BCE After the death of Solomon, the kingdom is divided into Israel in the north (present-day

Samaria) and Judah in the south, with its capital in Jerusalem.

701 BCE Judah devastated by Assyrian invasion. Jerusalem, led by King Hezekiah and inspired by the prophet Isaiah, remains unconquered.

627–586 BCE Prophet Jeremiah predicts doom in Jerusalem.

586 BCE Nebuchadnezzar destroys Jerusalem and the Temple of Solomon. End of the First Temple period. Jews exiled to Babylon.

540 BCE Babylon defeated by the Persians. Jews allowed to return to Jerusalem.

515 BCE Second Temple built upon the ruins of Solomon's Temple in Jerusalem.

332 BCE Alexander the Great conquers Judea; the Hellenistic era begins.

167 BCE Antiochus IV desecrates the Jerusalem temple and outlaws the Jewish religion.

164 BCE Judah Maccabee captures Jerusalem; temple rededicated. Judea becomes independent under the Maccabee (Hasmonean) dynasty.

63 BCE Judea incorporated into the Roman Empire.

8–4 BCE Jesus is born in Bethlehem.

62 CE Completion of the Herodian renovation of the Second Temple.

66–73 CE Jewish revolt against Rome. Jerusalem and the Second Temple captured by Rome and razed; Masada falls.

132 CE Second Revolt against Rome led by Bar Kokhba. The ruins of Jerusalem are freed; temple service resumes.

135 CE Bar Kokhba rebellion quelled. Emperor Hadrian orders Jerusalem rebuilt as Aelia Capitolina, a Roman city forbidden to Jews.

313–326 CE Emperor Constantine recognizes Christianity as the new religion of the Roman Empire. His mother, Queen Helena, visits the Holy Land to identify sites of Jesus's life and ministry.

326–614 CE Hundreds of Byzantine churches and monastic communities are built. Byzantine rulers impose restrictions against Jews.

614–629 CE Jerusalem conquered by the Persians, recaptured by the Byzantines.

638 CE Omar Ibn El Khattab conquers Jerusalem for Islam.

691 CE Dome of the Rock built on the Temple Mount.

720 CE Al Aqsa Mosque built on the Temple Mount.

1008 Caliph Al Hakim destroys churches and prevents Christian pilgrimage.

1099 Crusaders conquer Jerusalem. Muslims and Jews are massacred.

1187 Saladin (Saleheddin) recaptures Jerusalem from the Crusaders.

1240 Turkish armies plunder Jerusalem.

1267 Post-Crusader Jewish community reestablished in Jerusalem.

1291 Mameluke's conquest of Jerusalem.

1517 Ottoman Turkish conquest of Jerusalem.

1538 Ottoman sultan Suleiman the Magnificent orders the walls of Jerusalem rebuilt. These are the walls we see today.

1841 The first Protestant mission opens in Jerusalem.

1863 The first Hebrew newspaper.

1882 First wave of Jewish immigration from Europe and Yemen.

1917 The Balfour Declaration supports a Jewish national home in Palestine; the British free Jerusalem from the Turks.

1920 Official start of the British Mandate government of Jerusalem, Palestine.

1929 Arab-Jewish riots spark decades of intermittent skirmishes.

1948 The United Nations votes to partition Palestine into a Jewish state and an Arab state. The state of Israel declared, with Jerusalem as its capital. The city is surrounded and besieged by Arab armies.

1949 Cease-fire. Jerusalem is divided between Israel and Jordan. Jews are expelled from the Old City and forbidden to pray at the Western Wall. The Jewish cemetery on the Mount of Olives is desecrated, synagogues in the Jewish Quarter are demolished.

1967 Israel wins the Six-Day War, retakes all of Jerusalem, and institutes freedom of worship for all at Jewish, Christian, and Muslim holy sites.

1987 The First Palestinian intifada. Years of terrorist bombings begin to plague Jerusalem.

1994 Israel cedes Jericho and grants Bethlehem (just 13km/8 miles from Jerusalem) autonomy, as a first step toward peace with Palestinians.

2000 Second intifada hits Jerusalem hard; many downtown restaurants and establishments close as tourists stay away and Israelis stay home at night.

2007–2009 Tourism returns to Israel at near-record levels, then slumps slightly as a result of the world economic crisis.

2009 Jerusalem's population reaches 760,000 (70% Jewish, 30% Muslim and Christian Arab), constituting 10% of Israel's population. Nearly half of the city's Jewish population is religiously observant; 25% are ultra-Orthodox.

Useful Hebrew Words & Phrases

English is widely spoken in Jerusalem, and most street, restaurant, hotel, and store signs are in English, as well Hebrew or Arabic. A few words are the same in Hebrew and English—Internet, telephone, manicure—so it never hurts to try.

Fortunately, West Jerusalem and much of East Jerusalem uses the same numerals as in English-speaking countries: 1, 2, 3, 4, and so on.

Hebrew is a guttural language and has one sound, with soft and hard variations, that comes from the back of the throat, like the "ch" in the Scottish word "loch" or the German "achtung." In transliteration from Hebrew, you use "kh" to indicate this sound.

Helpful Words

Jerusalem	y'roo-sha-lye-im
Excuse me.	slee-kha
Yes.	kain
No.	lo
Please.	b'vah-kah-sha
Thank you.	to-dah
Thank you very much.	to-dah rah-bah
You're welcome.	b'vah-kah-sha
room	kheder
toilet	shayrooteem
bill	khesh-bon
there is	yesh
there isn't	ain
little	ktzat
much	har-beh
enough	mas-peek
very	me-od
good	tov
hot	khomm
bad	rah

Greetings

Hello.	sha-lom
Goodbye.	sha-lom
Good night.	lye-la tov
Good morning.	bo-ker tov
Good evening.	erev tov
See you later.	le-hit-rah-oat

Pronouns

I	ah-nee
you	ah-tah (ott for a woman)
he	hoo
she	hee
we	an-nakh-noo
this	zeh

Questions

where is?	ay-fo?
Where is a toilet?	ay-fo ha-shayrooteem?
Where is a telephone?	ay-fo telephone?
What?	mah?
What is this?	mah zeh?
When?	mah-tye?
Which bus number?	eh-zeh mispar autoboos?
What time is it?	ma ha-sha-ah?

Which?	*eh-zeh?*
how much?	*ka-mah?*
How much is it?	*ka-mah zeh oh-leh?*
how long?	*kama-zman?*

Language

English	*ahng-leet*
Hebrew	*ee-vreet*
I do not understand.	*ah-nee lo may-veen*

Emergency

police	*mish-tarah*
ambulance	*om-boo-lonce*
doctor	*roe-feh*
dentist	*roe-feh sheen-eye-yim*
hospital	*bet khoa-leem*

Places

central bus station	*takhana mer-ka-zeet*
store	*kha-noot*
synagogue	*bait k'ness-et*
bank	*banc*
hotel	*mah-lon*

Transport & Directions

Ben-Gurion Airport	*not-bogg*
station	*ta-kha-nah*
railroad	*rah-keh-vet*
bus	*auto-boos*
bus stop	*ta-kha-naht auto-boos*
taxi	*toxee*
meter (taxi)	*moa-neh*
shared taxi van *(sherut)*	*shay-root*
straight ahead	*ya-shar*
street	*r'khov*
near	*ka-rov*
far	*rah-khok*
stop here	*ah-tsor kahn*
to the right	*y'meen-ah*
to the left	*smol-ah*
wait	*reg-gah*

Restaurants & Food

restaurant	*miss-ah-dah*
cafe	*bet-ca-fe*
menu	*taf-reet*
breakfast	*ah-roo-khat bo-ker*

lunch	*ah-roo-chat tsa-ha-rye-im*
dinner	*ah-roo-chat erev*
waiter	*mel-tsar*
waitress	*mel-tsareet*
water	*my-im*
ice cream	*glee-dah*
wine	*yah-yin*
meat	*bah-sahr*
milk	*kha-lav*
ice	*kerakh*
salt	*me-lakh*
sugar	*sue-car*
tea	*tay*
coffee	*cafe*
bread	*lekhem*
salad	*sal-ott*

Days & Time

Sunday	*yom ree-shon*
Monday	*yom shay-nee*
Tuesday	*yom shlee-shee*
Wednesday	*yom reh-vee-ee*
Thursday	*yom kha-mee shee*
Friday	*yom shee-shee*
Saturday	*sha-baht*
minute	*da-kah*
hour	*sha-ah*
day	*yom*
week	*sha-voo-ah*
year	*sha-nah*
today	*hah-yom*
tomorrow	*ma-khar*
yesterday	*et-mohl*

Useful Arabic Words & Phrases

Useful Terms

please	*min fadlak*
thank you	*shoo-khraan*
hello	*a-halan, mahr-haba*
goodbye	*salaam aleikum, ma-ah-salameh*
right	*yemina*
left	*she-mal*

straight	doo-ree
today	il-yaum
tomorrow	boo-kra
what is your name?	shoo ismak?
my name is . . .	ismay . . .
how much is this?	ah-desh ha dah?

Measures & Numbers

one kilo	wahad kilo
half kilo (500 grams)	noos kilo
100 grams	mia gram
1	wa-had
2	ti-neen
3	talatay
4	ar-bah
5	ham-she
6	sitteh
7	sabah
8	tamanyeh
9	tay-sa
10	a-sha-rah
50	ham-seen
100	mia

Useful Websites

Airlines

AIR CANADA
www.aircanada.com
AIR FRANCE
www.airfrance.com
ALITALIA
www.alitalia.com
AMERICAN AIRLINES
www.aa.com
BRITISH AIRWAYS
www.ba.com
CONTINENTAL AIRLINES
www.continental.com
DELTA AIRLINES
www.delta.com
EGYPT AIR
www.egyptair.com

EL AL AIRLINES
www.elal.co.il
IBERIA AIRLINES
www.iberia.com
ISRAIR AIRLINES
www.israirairlines.com
LUFTHANSA
www.lufthansa.com
QANTAS AIRWAYS
www.qantas.com
SOUTH AFRICAN AIRWAYS
www.flysaa.com
SWISS AIR
www.swiss.com
TURKISH AIRLINES
www.thy.com

UNITED AIRLINES
www.united.com
US AIRWAYS
www.usairways.com

Car-Rental Agencies

AVIS
www.avis.com
BUDGET
www.budget.com
HERTZ
www.hertz.com
THRIFTY
www.thrifty.com

Index

See also Accommodations and Restaurant indexes, below.

Photo **Credits**

Notes